Behind the Pulpit

I Still Remember...

by

Sanedria Arne Potter

First published by AuthorHouse 05/29/04

ISBN: 1-4184-2721-7 (Paperback)

Printed in the United States of America
Bloomington, IN

This book is printed on acid free paper.

Dedication

To all Veterans who are still struggling to live a normal life. You are appreciated and not forgotten.

To all the Battered Women Shelters, you really make a difference and save lives. Thank you.

Also to everyone who had a less than storybook childhood. You can make it!

Last but not least to Jaelen Addison Miller, my two year old son. Thank you for letting Mommy write. I love you so much!

Acknowledgements

First and foremost I thank God for his many blessings.

Also great appreciation to:

My Mother, Sandra McNeal for not giving up. I love you.

My sisters and brothers; Carlette, Mia, Carl II, Joel, and Kelly. Thank you for all your support while I wrote this book. I appreciate all of your suggestions and ideas. Also I congratulate all of you for leading positive lives in spite of our childhood. Also to my brother Major Carlos, I am desperately searching and trying to find you. We all love you and miss you dearly. I know that one day we will reunite. You have three older sisters and three older brothers in your corner. Keep your head up, wherever you are.

My special friends and loved ones; Cedric, Tamika, Nekia, Mrs. Cheryl, Stephanie, Yvonne, Anthanette, Zena, all my Aunts, Uncles, and cousins. There is no way that I can list all the special people in my life. I have been blessed with so many. I love you all.

A very special thanks to Travis Hunter, author of 'Married But Still Looking' and 'Trouble Man'. When you could not even pronounce my first name you still extended a helping hand. Thanks for all the advice and referrals. You are the best.

To Porshe Foxx of V-103 in Atlanta, Ga. for rocking my box, and reminding me to "Make my Haters, My Motivators". Thank you girl!

To Jaelen, my only child, my son, my baby. Mommy loves you so much. Thank you for putting up with me while I was writing. Even at 2 years old, you have so much character and I am amazed that you are mine.

Daddy, Daddy, Daddy. What can I say? It's so difficult to say those three words. I will say that everyday

I try to understand you and your life. Also thank you for 'Dollar Fridays', it meant a lot to me.

To all my readers, thank you for your support.

How My Parents Met

June 1965

Sharon Johnson was happy to be at the Kennedy School Summer Dance. Even though it would be another year before she was in Jr. High, her older cousin Catherine had let her tag along. She had laid out all three of her good dresses. The black dress made the final cut. It was two seconds from being handed down to her younger sister Jean, but Sharon liked the way it looked.

The gymnasium was getting crowded, and little beads of sweat were forming under Sharon's arms. All the guys seemed tall and very different from the boys at her school. The music was blaring, and had her in a daze. So lost in the moment, she nearly spilled her punch, when a tall slim guy walked up, and asked her to dance. After accepting, the tall guy whisked her away to the dance floor. They danced three songs before another word was spoken.

When they finally took a break, Sharon learned that the tall guy was named Carlos Porter. He was in the ninth grade, and three years older than she was. She wondered what this older guy saw in her, but was thrilled at the same time. Neither of them had a phone, so they agreed to meet at the library on Saturday.

Catherine had been looking for Sharon all night, and finally found her in the corner hugging a tall guy.

"What are you doing hugging Carlos?" she asked after he left.

"You know him?"

"Who doesn't know Carlos, and his crazy family," Catherine responded.

3 years later

Carlos had decided to end his high school career. Even though it was his last year, he was fed up. His family did not have much money, and he was always being picked on for having to wear his father's much larger clothes. He decided to go to the military. Since he was only seventeen, his Mother had to sign for him. Three years went by, while he served in the Vietnam War.

Sharon was so in love, and counted the days until Carlos's next letter. They wrote each other all the time. He would send her beautiful poems. She would sit at his parent's house, and wait for his weekly phone call. She longed for the day when he would be home for good. Her free time was spent singing, and attending church. The local talent show circuit knew her name well. First place prize was always hers.

3 years later

Carlos was being discharged, just as Sharon was about to embark on a full scale singing career.

When he got home she was so happy. Now, her life would be complete. She had moved into her first apartment, and bought a used car. Her life was on track.

When Carlos asked Sharon if he could move in, she suggested that they get married. Her religious beliefs made her not want to shack up. He agreed, and they were married at the courthouse downtown.

It was a while before Sharon noticed that Carlos had went to the war, but an angry stranger had come back. He was very jealous, and did not like the attention singing gave her. When she was offered a recording contract, he made her decline it. He did start attending church with her, and that made Sharon happy.

1 year later

Carlos gathered his entire family in the living room of his Mother's house. Once he had everyone's attention he announced, "God has called me to preach. I will obey, and preach his word."

Sharon smiled. The thought of Carlos preaching, and her being a first lady was exciting. As she hugged him in the living room that day, the pain in her side was barely noticeable. *Now that he will be a preacher, I am sure he will keep his word, and not hit me anymore.*

Chapter 1

Christmas morning '84 I was awakened, not by the smells of cinnamon rolls and hot chocolate, but by a cold draft underneath my tattered nightgown. Even the two extra bodies that I shared the small bed with, could not keep the cold air out that morning. The body heat, I heard my aunts speak about, that black folks were to supposed to generate, was on strike that morning. I raised up to look around the dimly lit room. My older sister, Carla, and my younger sister, Mya, were still asleep. I peered over to the twin bed beside ours, and my two baby brothers were still snoring. Jason had his feet in Carlos Jr.'s face. At nine years old, I was very excited about Christmas.

"It's Christmas! It's Christmas! Wake up," I said to my sisters.

Carla had the worst breath in the morning, so I quickly turned my head as she let out her morning yawn.

Carlos Jr. and Jason did not wake up. My sisters and I ran to the living room. I got there first, and stood in the doorway of the living room frozen.

"Move out of the way Sharon. What are you doing?" Carla asked, as she pushed past me into the living room. By this time there were tears in my eyes. I could not believe it.

"We've been robbed," Mya shrieked.

Carla and I just looked at each other. We were a little older and knew the real deal. We had just gotten the water turned back on a couple of days before. Although I knew things had been tough lately, nothing could prepare me for this. Under the shabby Christmas tree, that we had so much fun putting up for the sixth year in a row, there was absolutely nothing. The only thing we saw was an old white sheet that we put there every year instead of a real tree skirt. Mya ran crying into my parents' room.

"Daddy, Daddy, our toys are gone!"

I did not hear Daddy say anything, but I could hear Momma trying to console Mya.

When he emerged from the bedroom he was fully dressed. He peered at us from the doorway. Carla and I both sat straight up, and tried to change our facial expressions.

Daddy was very strict. He was a preacher at a small church in Winston, North Carolina. We automatically were at attention at all times in his presence. You never knew what mood he would be in, so we were usually very quiet. Daddy served in the Vietnam War, and he was a very strange man. Momma said sometimes he would wake up from dreams, and command everyone to get down on the floor or rock the entire bed with his right leg, which would always shake at night. I would always hear people say he was exposed to some orange chemical, and that he was shell shock. Not knowing what that meant, I thought everybody's Daddy was like mine. He had a metal plate in his head from being shot, and I thought that sometimes it moved around, and made him go crazy.

That Christmas morning he just stood there looking at us like we did something wrong. We were just kids. Without saying a word to us, he went out the front door.

As soon as we heard the old Cadillac pull off, Carla and I jumped off the couch, and went to Momma's room.

Momma was a good person, and she would always try to make the best of suituations. I was named after her, and we had a special bond. She was a very good singer, who gave up a record deal to be a wife and Mother. I often wondered if she was happy. We got really bad whippings when we were out of line or if Daddy thought we needed one. Although I think Momma was too afraid to make him stop beating us, she would always sneak into our room later and check our legs for whips and bruises. She would tell us everything was going to be ok.

That day Momma sat on the edge of the bed, with her hair a mess, all over her head. She looked really tired and old that morning, and I could tell she had been crying. As usual, making us feel better was on her mind.

"Things are a little tight right now, and I need for you all to be big girls and Mommy will get you something next week."

Carla and I nodded in unison, and hugged Momma really tight. I pretended to understand, but really tears were about to surface. Christmas had been on my mind for a long time. We never got much, but still I had spent the previous weeks imagining what would be under the tree. Mya was fast asleep on Momma's lap with white dried up tears on her face. We just sat there on the bed, and she sang us a song.

When she finished, we felt a little better. Momma began to tell us a funny story about when she was growing up. This peaceful moment was suddenly interrupted by the sound of Daddy's old Cadillac. The click clack of the muffler startled me. I nearly fell off the bed. We quickly wiped our faces, and ran to our room. As we closed the bedroom door, the boys were waking up. Carlos Jr. was six, and Jason was five. They repeated our initial excitement of Christmas morning. Just then I became sad again. For them understanding would not be an option. At that age, I am sure they would be heart broken.

"Carla... Sharon... Carlos Jr.... Jason yall come here," Daddy yelled.

Scared to death, we all went to the living room. Mya was already there, and met us at the doorway.

"Look Sharon, Daddy got me a Candyland game!"

She was ecstatic, and smiling from ear to ear. The dried up tears were still on her face. I looked around the room, and there were five separate piles of gifts. Some were half wrapped, and some were not wrapped at all. I did not care. They were gifts. Daddy showed us which pile belonged to whom. My sisters and I had board games, and little rag dolls. The boys had trucks, and G. I. Joe men. Everyone was happy, and Dad even smiled a little bit. We all sang songs, and Momma fixed breakfast. Carlos and Jason never knew what had happened Christmas morning 1984, and we soon forgot about it also.

****

The first day of school after Christmas break, all the kids would wear new outfits they got as gifts. I never had new clothes, so I always tried to be creative with what I had. Momma made most of our clothes, and the rest were second hand. Whenever we would see something that we liked, she would say, "I can make that."

As I approached the bus stop, I could hear Marsha Davis, the neighborhood bully, giggling and pointing. She was always picking on someone. Carla and I were on the top of her list. Sometimes my Daddy would come to the bus stop with us, and make all the kids stand in a single file line, until the bus came. He also let them know that he was a preacher, and did not allow his children to fight. 'Turn the other cheek' was Daddy's motto. He told all the kids to let him know if they ever saw us fighting, and that gave Marsha ultimate power over us. She would torture us, and had made a game out of thumping us in the head. That day I had made up my mind that if she did it to me, I was going to bust her in the mouth and take my punishment from Daddy. I thought my latest creation of two outfits mixed was cute, and I wanted to know what she was snickering about. A quick glance behind me answered the question. There, on our front porch, was Momma putting Mya's coat on. Her hair was all over her head. She had on a nightgown, and boy tube socks with stripes on them. She saw me looking, and waved. Even though everyone knew who she was, I continued to the bus stop without returning the wave. The one good thing about

Momma being on the porch was that Marsha would not be thumping anybody's head.

The ride to school seemed longer than normal today. Our school was in the next town. It was about a thirty-minute ride. I was in the fourth grade, and Carla was in the fifth. We were only ten months apart. Every year we stayed the same age for two months. Mya was in the second grade, and Carlos Jr. was in the first. Jason had not started school yet, because his birthday was too late in the year. Carla and I always sat together on the bus, and played tic-tac-toe. Mya and Carlos usually went back to sleep.

That morning, Marsha spent the entire ride running her mouth about all the cool things she got. As the bus pulled in the parking lot, I could see all the new outfits, coats, hats, lunchboxes, and bookbags. I did get some new pencils that came in a beautiful box, so I put them on top of my schoolbooks, and walked into Kernersville Elementary School.

Mrs. White's fourth grade class was full of chatter that morning. Everyone was discussing what he or she got for Christmas. I went to my assigned seat, and began putting my books away. My shiny new pencil box was proudly left on top of my desk. No one really talked to me, and my friends were few. I was a good student, and always made the honor roll. Mrs. White must have known what I was going through, and always made sure that she said a kind word or praised me for something.

"That is a fancy pencil box you have there Ms. Porter," she said.

She was a great teacher, and lifted my spirits many days.

I gave her a big smile and said, "My Daddy bought it for me for Christmas."

"No he didn't," I heard from across the room. Everyone turned around in the direction from which this voice came. Up against the wall, all decked out in a new outfit and hairdo, was Francis Rock. She was my first cousin. My Daddy and her Mom were brother and sister. Her Dad had a really good job, and they always had the best of everything. We got along o.k., but I knew she thought she was better than my sisters and I. She got that attitude from her Mom. With the entire class giving her their full attention, she continued.

"Her Daddy came to our house Christmas morning. He asked my Mother for some of our unwanted, small gifts, because they didn't have anything for Christmas."

"That is enough Ms. Rock," Mrs. White interrupted.

"Well it's true, we gave him all the stuff we didn't want," Francis blurted out shamelessly.

That is why the gifts were half wrapped and some were not wrapped at all. It never crossed my mind where the gifts came from. We were just happy to get them. At that moment the entire class seemed to be laughing at me. Mrs. White tried to calm everyone down.

"You are no longer my cousin," I said, and ran out of the class.

I was horrified, and could not believe Francis had done that to me. My heart sank to my knees.

How could my Daddy go to those uppity people, and ask them for anything. I would have rather had nothing for Christmas. It is amazing that we were so happy with our gifts, and they were all things the Rock kids did not want.

Francis made me feel really low. The girls' bathroom was the first place I saw. Luckily all the stalls were empty. I slid down the wall, and crouched by the radiator. *If I hold my arm on here long enough to burn, maybe they will send me home. I ought to just jump out of the window.*

As I stood up, and peered out the window, I began to imagine all sorts of bad things happening to Francis. Like her falling in the mud during recess, and messing up that nice new outfit. Or somehow gum getting stuck in her hair, and her having to get it all cut off.

"Sharon, are you all right?"

Mrs. White had found me. She persuaded me to come back to class. The kids had settled down, and a couple of them actually talked to me. It seems that Mrs. White had had a conversation with them about what Christmas was really about. I avoided eye contact with Francis for the rest of the day. On the ride home I told Carla what had happened.

"I'm throwing my gifts in the trash when I get home," she said.

We decided not to tell Mya or Carlos Jr. As we walked in the door Jason ran up to us, with one of his Christmas gifts in tow. I burst into tears, and went to tell my Momma what happened. As I finished my story, a strange look came over her face. I quickly glanced behind me, and saw Daddy standing in the doorway. To this day I don't know if he had heard what I said. All I know is that I felt something come down across my back. I tumbled to the floor, and rolled up in a defensive ball. I looked up just as the old extension cord was coming down again. Daddy continually struck me. Each hit worse than the last.

"Carlos wait," Momma said.

"You better hush your mouth Sharon, before your next," Daddy threatened. "You don't ever talk bad about family. You don't deny your family. Do... you... hear... me?" Daddy screamed, timing each word with a hard blow to my back, legs, or whatever body part he made contact with.

"But Daddy," I tried to explain.

"I don't want to hear anything from you," he said.

With each hit I thought: *What did I do? Why didn't I just jump? I hate my life.*

Francis had went home, and told her mother that I was at school denying that she was my cousin. Of course she hadn't mentioned that she told the whole class that we had gotten their unwanted toys for Christmas. My uppity Aunt Genene, who probably felt like I should be proud to even know her children, immediately summoned my Daddy to her house. She confronted him about my comments. He then came home, and without a single word, began to give me one of the worst beatings I ever had. Not once did he ask me for my side of the story. Instead, he just added to my pain and humiliation.

I could barely walk after that beating. As I lay in my bed, thoughts of running away filled my head. My legs were bleeding, and I could feel the swelling. A short time later I heard Daddy's car pull off. Like clockwork Momma rushed in, and began checking my legs, and making sure I was all right.

"Things are going to get better. Just pray," Momma said.

The song she sang, as she cleaned my wounds, was beautiful. I never understood how Momma dealt with it. She never seemed happy. I think that is why she would rarely comb her hair or why she did not care what she wore. Our happiness was important to her, though. She really tried to give us little rays of hope. I laid in Momma's arms, and although it was still daylight, I went to sleep.

Chapter 2

"Let the Church say Amen," Elder Porter commanded to his tiny congregation.

"Amen," the church responded.

First Prayer Church of God was in a small house, which was converted into a church. There were about thirty members including my family. Daddy was the pastor. Momma was the first lady and organist. She only knew a couple of chords, so the choir, which was made up of Carla, Mya, Carlos Jr., Jason and myself mostly sang acapello. Momma could sing, so naturally we had good voices, and did very well. Daddy could sing also, and we often sang at different churches as a family. During those times life did not seem so bad. He played the guitar, and would often make up songs for us to sing.

Behind the pulpit Daddy was a different person. He was an eloquent speaker, and preached great sermons. The entire congregation thought the world of him. He was often invited to other churches to speak. The way he shouted, and praised the Lord, was the talk of the town. It was nothing for Daddy to catch the spirit, and run around the church or do a full split in the aisle. To the outside world, we probably appeared to be a normal family, and for brief moments it seemed true. That is, until something would trigger Daddy to flip out. Then we either got a whipping or were forced to endure one of his weird forms of punishment, like standing in the corner on one leg or kneeling on rice. Sometimes the anger would not be taken out on us. Those times Daddy would jump on Momma. She got severe beatings just like we did.

Daddy's sermon was especially long today, and I was tired. I wondered how he could be so pumped up after keeping us up last night. He yelled, and screamed all night about the importance of being ready for God's return. Ironically parts of his sermon today made reference to what he was stressing last night. M*aybe he was practicing on us.*

"God is coming back for a church without a spot or wrinkle," Daddy shouted as I mouthed the same words along with him. I must have really lost myself in mocking him, because next thing I knew he was coming towards me. *Did he see me?* I thought as he came closer to me, still swaying in the spirit.

"God is coming soon," he said just inches from me.

"Will you be ready?" Daddy asked the church as he thumped me in my head the way Marsha does us at the bus stop.

"Will you be ready?" he repeated. Daddy did a Micheal Jackson spin, and a James Brown slide, and was headed back to the pulpit before I knew what hit me. Keeping still after that was hard. It was a sure thing that Daddy was going to whip my butt when we got home. I was rocking in the pew and crying. The sobbing was so hard that the usher gave me some tissue, and began to fan me. She thought I had caught the spirit. What I had caught, was the vision of the old extension cord that Daddy used to whip us. I was so tired of getting beatings, and thought that I had had more than enough. Thinking of a way to get out of this was my next concern. Up until the end of the service, my thinking cap was on.

After the service, while Daddy was putting his bible away, I walked straight up to him.

"That was a great sermon. I remembered what you said last night and I was just repeating it with you."

As we stood there, I hoped my words were convincing. Before I could find out, one of the ushers interrupted.

"Elder Porter, Sister Mable is requesting prayer."

Daddy was whisked off to the rear of the church. I don't know if my act worked. He had not responded to me. Thank God for good ole Sister Mable. Every other week she had a different ailment. I quickly ran outside where my brothers and sisters were. Momma was already in the car. Daddy would always be the last one to leave the church. He talked with every person, and prayed for anyone that requested it. Sometimes we would stay after the service for another hour or more. Daddy would yell at Momma for not being at his side during these prayers. She would explain that the younger kids needed tending to, but really, I think it was hard for her to back him up. Especially knowing the real deal about his character and all.

When Daddy finally came to the car, he was quiet. After starting the engine, and adjusting the volume on the radio, he pulled off. We headed in the opposite direction of our house.

"Carlos, where are we going?"

"There is a birthday dinner today at Genene's for Mom," Daddy said. "Yall kids need to remember your home training."

"Yes Sir," we said in unison.

Even though it still hurt me, acting funny towards Francis would not be a smart move. I had escaped one beat down today, and definitely did not want to stir up any trouble.

Grandma Florida was seventy years old, and still as beautiful as a young lady. She had long black hair that came to the middle of her back. Too bad none of that good hair was passed along to us. Ronald was Daddy's father. For some reason, everybody called him Ronald. Whenever I called him Grandpa, my cousins would laugh at me. The entire family feared this man. He was a true patriarch of his family. If Ronald did not want something to happen, it did not happen.

Momma did not look happy. Daddy never told her anything in advance. He never considered if she had something to do. What if she already had something planned? As we pulled up to the overly decorated house, I saw the Thumson's. They included my Aunt Brenda, her husband Lionel, and their two daughters Rayna and Tasha. Rayna was older than I was, but Tasha was my age, and nice. She did not act funny towards us and I liked her. Both my cousins were dressed really cute. That was not a surprise. My Aunts were always in competition with each other about their daughters. Aunt Genene has another daughter older than Francis named Mona. She made sure her girls always wore the latest fashions, and although Aunt Brenda didn't have nearly as much money, she managed to keep up. Even though Tasha was a little overweight, if Francis had on a mini skirt, you best believe Aunt Brenda would be squeezing Tasha into one. It was very amusing. Aunt Genene also has one son, named Harry after his Daddy.

Uncle Timothy was also amongst the crowd at Grandma's. He had no wife, an about 10 children. None of his kids would be there though. He put the "d" in deadbeat, but women could not get enough of him. Uncle Timothy was way to friendly for me, so I tried to avoid him. Something wasn't right about all those hugs and kisses, and him always wanting you to sit on his lap.

Grandma was sitting on the porch in a rocking chair, looking as pretty as she pleased. I loved her so much, and she never mistreated us. She always gave us peppermint from her purse. Even though they sometimes tasted like perfume, it meant alot to me. I ran to Grandma as soon as I got out of the car, and gave her a hug. The tightness of my grip probably puzzled her. If she only knew the pain that we were going through. *Or did she know?* Momma did not get to see her family that much. When she did, she kept our problems to herself. But my Daddy's side had to know. He would flip out on them too. If he got mad, the windows and doors of their houses were in trouble.

I hoped that today would go well, but this is the family that can't get along for two seconds. We never have family reunions for that very reason. *Maybe they were turning over a new leaf?*

"Where all these nappy head children come from?"

I did not have to turn around to know that it was Uncle Bud. Whenever this man was around, you were bound to have a good time. He had diabetes, and had to have one of his arms amputated, but he was full of life and hilarious. His longtime girlfriend Tangerine had a small convenience store. Even though she had epilepsy, she was still very functional, and they ran the store together. They had two kids Cheryl and Ronald Porter III. Uncle Bud was Ronald Porter II. He always had some candy or snacks for us, and was my favorite uncle.

The table was spread out real nice with all kinds of good food. Aunt Genene was real superstitious about eating other people's cooking, so she prepared everything herself. There were barbecue ribs, steaks, macaroni and cheese, collard greens, potato salad and rolls. She also had baked a couple of pies and cakes. When she announced that it was time to eat, everyone hurried to get in line. Tasha ended up ahead of Francis in line.

"You need to get behind me Piggy," Francis said, referring to the fact that Tasha was a little chubby. Francis thought since it was her front yard, she should be in front.

"I was here first and it's Miss Piggy to you," Tasha shot back.

A big argument started between the two 9 year old kids. Aunt Brenda rushed over to see what the commotion was all about.

"Everyone has to stand in line, Francis," she explained.

"I'm scared Miss Piggy gon' eat all the food," Francis said, getting smart with Aunt Brenda.

"You better watch your mouth," Aunt Brenda said, raising her hand as if she was going to spank her.

"If you hit me, I gon' tell my Momma!"

"I'm not scared of you, or your Momma. If she would whip you sometimes, you wouldn't have such a smart mouth."

Out of no where Aunt Genene comes to the table, and immediately begins to fuss at Aunt Brenda. Things got real heated. As usual they start revealing each other's business for any ears that would listen.

"Don't worry about what I do with my child. You need to worry about getting out of Momma's house and getting your own place. They are tired of you being there, and you got a sorry husband living there with you. What kind of man is that?" Aunt Genene said with her hands on her hips.

"What kind of man let's his wife beat on him? Tell me that! He only bought you this house, because he's scared to say no to you. Instead of beating your husband, you need to be disciplining those bad kids of yours."

"No you didn't," Aunt Genene said ready to fight.

"Yes I did," Aunt Brenda shot back.

It got real ugly out there. Ronald was trying to make peace. Grandma was still sitting on the porch rocking. Uncle Harry was very quiet, knowing that Aunt Brenda was telling the truth. I glanced at Momma, and we both had a good laugh. Anytime my snooty Aunts made a fool out of themselves; we would laugh to ourselves. They thought they were so better than we were, but they always ended up looking stupid. Francis and Tasha were gone from the table by now, but these crazy ladies were still talking about abortions, shoplifting and all kinds of private affairs. The funny thing about the Porter family is that, they beat each other to death, but no one outside the family better do it. If something happens to someone in this family, the whole crew shows up, ready to throw down.

They argued so much they set Daddy off. He began to preach at the top of his lungs. When he lost his voice, he started jumping, and breaking windows. It was so crazy, and so typical of the Porters. That is the very reason why anywhere you go in our town, everybody knows the Porter Family. Even though I was only nine, I could hardly wait until I got married so my last name could change.

Chapter 3

It was the day after Easter when Momma got the news about her Dad, George Johnson. He had Alzheimer's, and his condition had gotten really bad. It was to the point that he would not eat. Every time Grandma would try to feed him, he would bite her fingers. When Momma heard that he was in the hospital, she wanted to go see him. She knew this would cause an argument with Daddy, so she made sure everything in the house was in order. Then she prepared his favorite meal of chicken, and macaroni and cheese. Dinner tonight would be a family affair. We would all eat together most of the times, but the times Daddy would eat dinner in his room were the best meals we had. Anytime he ate at the table with us, he would monitor the way we chewed our food and critique our every move. He always said I chewed too fast, and ate like a dog. I really tried to eat the 'right' way. He made me nervous and uncomfortable. If we ate potato chips around him, we had to suck them until they got soft, and then chew them. Daddy could not stand to hear anyone eat anything, that would cause crunching or smacking.

"Momma, I'm hungry," Jason said.

We had been waiting on Daddy for almost three hours. It was fifteen minutes until our bedtime, and he had not come home yet. Momma went ahead, and gave us our dinner. All the silverware we had was raggedy, except for one spoon. It was silver, and really shiny. Every meal, there would be an argument about who was getting the 'big spoon'. When Daddy was at the table whoever grabbed it first had it. We knew better than to argue in front of him. That night I got in the kitchen first. I grabbed the spoon and licked it. That pretty much sealed my victory. We finished our meal, and got ready for bed. Daddy still had not come home.

I slept on the couch in the living room, now. The bed had gotten too small for my sisters and I to share. We were always complaining so Daddy made us decide which one of us would sleep in the living room. Neither Mya nor Carla would ever say anything, and when Daddy said decide he wanted an immediate decision. I did not want to get an undeserved beat down, so I made the couch my new bedtime friend. The cold and darkness of the living room was unkind to me. Nightmares were very frequent. I could not say anything though, for fear of what Daddy would do if I complained.

The sound of fumbling keys woke me. I could tell it was really late, because the slob on the side of my face was dried up, and my lip was sore. Some kids suck their thumb, but I had a bad habit of sucking my bottom lip. It would be swollen some mornings from me doing it in my sleep. The top row of my teeth stuck out farther than the bottom because of it. If it was sore that meant I had been asleep for a long time. Suddenly, thoughts of Grandpa came to mind. We never got to see him or Momma's family too much. I hoped that we would get to go.

"Where have you been?" Momma questioned Daddy, as he entered their bedroom.

"I've been out witnessing, and trying to bring souls to Christ."

"It is one o'clock in the morning, Carlos," Momma shot back, forgetting to be nice.

Just then I heard a loud crash. I wondered if the other kids had been awakened by the disturbance. The living room was right next to my parent's bedroom, so I heard a lot. Daddy and Momma were fighting. I pulled the covers over my head, and thought of ways to kill Daddy. These thoughts came often. Sometimes I would dream of how it would be done. This way of living was getting old.

After several loud crashes and screaming, all sounds from the other side of the door ceased. I thought that maybe Daddy had calmed down. Then I began to hear something again. At first I wasn't sure what it was. It sounded sort of muffled, like the sound you make when someone has his or her hand over your mouth. I also heard Daddy making this moaning sound off and on for a few minutes. The old bed in their room was making that squeaking noise again. Next I heard footsteps, and then water running in the bathroom sink. It must have been Daddy, because when I pulled the covers off my head I saw Momma in the doorway of their bedroom. She was looking to see if I was asleep. Our eyes met, and she was crying. Her face was swollen, and she looked real tired. The old nightgown, that once was nice, was ripped, and part of her breast was hanging out. She tried to hide her face, and disappeared into the kitchen. From the noises I heard, I could tell she was warming up Daddy a plate. *Didn't he just beat her? The last thing I would be doing was warming a plate.* I struggled for a lot of years to understand my home life.

****

Grandpa had been in the hospital for over a week, when we finally got to see him. Momma just sat at his bedside, and put her head in his lap, as if she was a little girl. I don't think he recognized any of us. Partly from the disease, and partly because he really did not know us. Grandma Mary was happy to see us. It made her day. I stared at her for awhile. She was my Grandma, but I did not know anything about her. Having a relationship with her and Grandpa was a dream of mine. The one thing I did know about her is that she could not stand Daddy, and was not afraid to let everyone know it. She was a church-going woman, but also a feisty woman. If something was on her mind it was voiced, and there was something she did not like about Daddy. "I'd rather see a black cat coming my way," she would say.

As Momma stood up to go to the bathroom, the bruise under her eye was almost invisible. That was the reason for the delay in coming to see Grandpa. For some reason Momma never told her family about Daddy's violence. I am sure my Uncle Teddy, Momma's brother, would have fixed Daddy up real good, had he known.

"Sharon, are you o.k., you don't look so good?" Grandma asked.

"I'm fine Momma, just a little tired," she answered just before fainting.

I ran to get the nurse. When I returned, Grandma was on the floor with Momma. She was really upset at what a closer inspection of her face had revealed. The anger at Daddy was very visible. Momma had come to, but she was silent. At Grandma's continued insistence the nurse checked her out.

We waited for what seemed like an eternity for her and the nurse to come back. When Momma came back she was exhausted, and just wanted to go home. Grandma wanted to know what the nurse had said.

"Did they say everything was alright baby?" Grandma asked.

"Everything is fine, Momma," she said softly, almost in a whisper.

"Well?"

"Well what Momma?" she responded much louder.

"When are you due?"

We all looked shocked. Jason was five years old, and we never thought about having another brother or sister.

"I am 5 weeks pregnant," Momma blurted out before she burst into tears.

"There is no use in crying about it now. What's done is done, but you need to make sure you take care of that, after this one. You are having it hard enough with the ones you got," Grandma said.

"I know Momma," she said gathering us together to leave.

"I've been dreaming about fish for the last few weeks but I never thought it was you," Grandma went on and on. This was a superstition of hers. She believed that whenever she dreamed of fish, someone in the family was pregnant.

"Bye Grandma," I said as we left the hospital.

Daddy was waiting outside for us in the old Cadillac. The news excited him, because twelve kids was his goal. He seemed oblivious to the fact that he could not take care of the ones he already had. Whenever Momma was pregnant, Daddy was almost nice. Although he would still yell and argue, he would not hit her. However, Momma was still sad. I don't think she wanted anymore children, but Daddy was strongly against birth control. So in between the fighting, the babies kept coming.

Chapter 4

Momma's stomach was getting bigger, and so was our congregation at the church. Every Sunday we would get new members. Our choir was also growing. A group of sisters had joined a couple of months prior. The flowered dresses they wore told of the deep country, which was their home. Bernice was the oldest of the three. The twenty-five year old woman with long legs and a full chest, wore her hair in a tight bun every Sunday. Quickly, she became involved in different aspects of the church. Being a new Christian made her eager to learn. Like many other members she admired her pastor. Elder Porter could do no wrong in her eyes. He would often visit her, in her home, for bible study.

Bernice would come over, and baby-sit if Momma had a doctor's appointment. Recently, it had been announced that the job of church secretary was hers. She came over to watch us right after she found out. The new position excited her, but trying to brush Jason's hair changed her mood. That was a hard task. If you brushed it, five minutes later it would be rolled back up. He was very tender headed.

"You hurting me, Ms. Bernice!"

"Sit still Jason."

Jason squirmed and moaned. He finally jumped up and ran. The sudden movement sent Bernice tumbling to the floor. Carla and I were laughing. Daddy came in just as she was getting up off the floor.

"What happened, Sister Bernice?" he said as he rushed over to help her up.

"Just trying to brush Jason's hair. You know how tender headed he is."

"Jason come in here," Daddy shouted.

"Yes sir," he answered shaking.

"You apologize to Sister Bernice."

"I'm sorry. It just hurt so bad."

"I want you to go in the corner and stand on one leg. If you drop your leg, you are going to be in big trouble."

Daddy had a mind full of weird punishments. Trying to remain on one leg is hard. You almost wished for the whipping. As Jason stood there with his arms stretched out trying to balance, I felt so bad for him. Even Bernice had a funny look on her face.

Momma came home a short while later, and Jason was still in the corner. By now he was trembling. Luckily Daddy had some witnessing to do, and he and Bernice left when she came.

Daddy did a lot of witnessing to lost souls. Bernice was always happy to accompany him. She really believed in him and his ministry. I could never tell if Momma liked Bernice or not. She was always with Daddy. I felt relieved that he was gone so much. He was even away from the house when Momma went into labor.

When Daddy got home that day, Bernice was with him.

"Daddy, Daddy, Momma is having the baby," Mya shrieked.

"Where is she?" Daddy asked.

"She called the ambulamb," Jason said.

Daddy rushed out of the door and left Bernice to watch us.

Kerry Emanuel Porter was born February 12th, 1986. He was a beautiful little boy. Now there were three girls, and three boys. Momma decided to take Grandma's advice, and end her childbearing career. So the next morning she signed for the procedure. As she was being carted off for the tubulization Daddy asked where she was going. When she told him, he flipped out. Just as he was about to be thrown out, Daddy left Momma and the baby in the hospital, and came home. I overheard him telling Bernice his version, but Momma told us what really happened, once she came home.

When Daddy got home I thought Bernice would be leaving, but she didn't. She hung around, and fixed him some dinner. I could hear them talking in the living room. Daddy was giving her a lesson on obedience. Later on, Bernice obeyed, and followed him into my Momma's bedroom. This time the sounds I heard were not muffled. In fact it was very clear, and equally disturbing to me, and I went and told Carla what was going on. We listened at the door for what seemed liked hours. I was sucking my lip intensely, and getting madder by the moment. When the bed stopped squeaking, we began to hear what sounded like praying.

"Lord please forgive us," Daddy said.

"Lord please forgive us," Bernice repeated.

"With our mind, body, and soul we do your will, Amen," Daddy said and Bernice repeated.

"You and I are doing God's will Bernice. Two clean sheets cannot become dirty. We are both clean for God. Do you understand that?" Daddy asked.

"Yes, Elder Porter," Bernice said.

Carla and I were shocked. How could Daddy do that to Momma? This was the same man, who preached about fornication and adultery.

The sound of approaching footsteps made us move from the door. We stayed out of the way the rest of the evening. I did not want to look at Daddy or Bernice. I could not wait to tell my Momma. Maybe she would leave.

The next morning Bernice was still there. She fixed our breakfast, and sent us off to school as if nothing was out of the ordinary. When we returned home, there they were. It was like she was in a trance, jumping at Daddy's every command. At night they would retire to Momma's bedroom with no shame.

The squeaking bed, and loud prayers, continued for two days. Daddy had not mentioned Momma, or been back to the hospital. We did not have a phone, so Momma could not call, and I was beginning to get worried.

"Daddy when is Momma coming home?" I asked.

He looked as if he had been jerked back into reality. I ran next door with him to use the phone.

"Can I have Mrs. Sharon Porter's Room?"

"One Moment Please," the nurse replied and placed Daddy on hold.

"I'm sorry, but she has been discharged," the nurse said after returning to the phone.

"What do you mean? I meant to say, when was she discharged? This is her husband," Daddy shouted.

"Hold on," she said.

"Mr. Porter," a different nurse, with a different tone said, "Mrs. Porter was released about three hours ago and the poor woman is still in the lobby with that beautiful baby waiting to be picked up."

Before Daddy could respond, the nurse slammed the phone down in his ear.

"Tell Bernice I will be right back," Daddy said as he cranked up the car, and went to pick up Momma.

Without telling Bernice a thing, I sat on the porch, and imagined a real man being there when he arrived. *The handsome prince would extend his hand to Momma and help her into a new Cadillac. They would pull up to our raggedy house, pick us up, and take us to our new home complete with a pool. He would never beat Momma, and only whip us when we were out of line.* The sound of a horn blowing ended my daydream. Daddy was waving for me to come help with the bags. So much for wishful thinking. I jumped off the porch and ran to the old car.

Kerry was a happy baby, and he brought Momma joy. She sat, and rocked Kerry, and sang wonderful songs to him. As we all gathered around to see the new bundle of joy, Daddy announced that he was going to take Bernice home.

"Thank you for helping out," Momma said to Bernice.

"Anytime Sister Porter," Bernice said and gave Momma a hug.

I almost fell out the chair I was sitting in. That lady actually hugged my Momma. Could she really believe that she was doing God's will by sleeping with my Daddy? I wanted to tell on Bernice, but I did not know how. Momma seemed happy for once in a long time, and I was not about to take that away from her.

Chapter 5

Bernice ended up telling on herself when her stomach began to grow. I guess Daddy was going to continue to reproduce where he could, since his wife had gotten her tubes tied. Bernice had to speak up about her child's father because she needed help. She was scared and alone. The poor woman really thought obeying her pastor was doing God's will. He had mind control over her because she was so impressionable. At least that is what I heard some ladies at church saying, when they didn't know I could hear them. My ears were always open. I even heard Daddy tell Bernice that as long as they got down on their knees and repented, it was o.k.

When Momma found out, she was furious. That was the final straw for her. It was time to leave. She had accepted the baby he had with someone else while they were dating, but now that they were married she would not be so understanding. I had heard about my oldest sister Diane, but we had never met her. I often thought about her. Daddy never saw her either, and that meant another child growing up without her father. Little did she know that with a Daddy like ours, she might be better off.

"Everybody's talking about who the father of Bernice's baby is," Momma said one Wednesday after returning home from choir rehearsal. "Kerry is eight months old, and Bernice is eight months pregnant. You must think I am stupid. I guess she was doing more than babysitting while I was in the hospital."

"Sharon, the baby is mine. It has happened now, and there is nothing you can do about it," Daddy said boldly. He didn't even try to lie.

"I am sick and tired of your mess Carlos. How much do you think I can take?" asked Momma as she shielded her face from the large fist that was closing in on her.

Daddy fought Momma for what seemed like hours. He pulled his belt off and began to whip her as if she was a child. When she fell to the ground, he stomped on her stomach and kicked her in her side. Kerry began to cry. He was sleep when we got home, but all the commotion had woke him up. Too scared to move, no one went to Kerry. He screamed and cried even louder. The scene was total chaos. I decided that I had to go get Kerry. Daddy was in a violent rage, and I was more scared for Kerry than myself. Carla and I tiptoed into the bedroom, and got him out of the homemade crib. He was soaking wet, and we could not find the diapers.

"Let's just go back to our bedroom," Carla whispered. "We'll figure something out."

Carla took the baby, and tried to quiet him. Carlos, Jason, and Mya had been hovered in the corner of the bedroom. They all ran over to Kerry, and attempted to pacify him.

"Take the diaper off of him Carla," I said.

"What are we going to put on him?" she asked.

"I don't know, but he can't stay wet, he's soaked," I replied.

Meanwhile, as Kerry was butt naked, but happy, Momma continued to be assaulted. She tried to get out of the door, but before she could, Daddy threw a match in her hair. The bright flames caught Kerry's attention. Her freshly greased mane burned and sizzled. The house smelled like a pressing comb. Momma sat in a frozen daze as what little hair she had melted away. She did not move. Something was wrong. Daddy was still ranting and raving, and we knew better than to get in his way. I tried to talk my brothers and sisters into jumping on him, but everyone was too scared. So as Daddy continued to yell, Momma continued to burn.

Suddenly, there was a knock on the door. Daddy, as if by magic, became a sane and normal man. He began to brush off his pants, and straighten his shirt. We had seen him do this so many times before, when the police would come, after one of the neighbors would hear the commotion.

"What the Hell?" asked Aunt Linda, when she burst into the house after seeing smoke seep from the window.

"This is a family matter Linda," Daddy said as he tried to push her out the door.

"Carlos you know you're dead wrong," Aunt Linda yelled at Daddy as she caught a glimpse of where the smoke was coming from. "You supposed to be a preacher, a man of God!"

Aunt Linda was my Daddy's half sister. They had the same father, but different mothers. That was one lady that was not afraid of the Elder. She told it like it was, and always looked out for us.

Aunt Linda ran and got a wet towel, and put it on Momma's head. It was just in time too, because after the fire was out, her hair was nearly down to the scalp on one side. It was an oblong bald section. Throughout the entire burning incident Momma had been motionless, in one spot. After the fire was out she still did not move.

Scared to utter a word, we all sat crouched at the door of the kitchen trying to keep the baby quiet. Daddy went to his room as if nothing happened, and Aunt Linda called the paramedics. She had stopped by on her way to work, so as she heard the sirens getting closer she said, "Everything will be o.k. now," and hesitantly left.

"We have a 10-40 with injuries at 437 Nash Street. We need police and ambulance to respond." Ronald heard the dispatcher say over the airwaves of his most prized possession. Ronald was dedicated to his scanner. It stayed on day and night. He always knew what was going on and where. Immediately recognizing his son's address, he sped to the scene. Even though he was seventy-six, and could hardly turn his body to look both ways, he still managed to drive. Arriving just seconds before, he quickly surveyed the scene, and took over the show when the police came. As if his aged eyes witnessed the whole disturbance, he spelled out a scenario that was far different than what had actually happened.

"They always get into little spats," Ronald said trying to minimize the situation. "Sharon starts fights with Carlos all the time," he continued trying to make Momma sound like less of a victim.

Momma was sitting on the couch. She was rocking back and forth and talking to herself. Daddy was well poised, and well spoken. He looked like the intelligent one, and Momma looked as if she had escaped from a mental institution.

Ronald manipulated the entire episode. By the time he was finished, the paramedics bandaged Momma's head and everybody left.

Once back in the house Daddy surprisingly ordered Momma to fix his dinner.

"Sure Carlos, is there anything else you need," she said in a sweet, catering voice.

Daddy did not answer. He just went into his room, and closed the door. I ran to the kitchen to check on Momma. I was shocked to find her preparing Daddy's food and singing.

"Ain't no need to worry, what the night is gonna bring. Cause it will be all over in the morning," Momma sang over and over in a quiet voice. I thought she had gone crazy. Even though she knew the entire song word for word, she just kept singing those lines.

"Do you need any help?" I offered not knowing if she even knew that I was there. She was acting really weird, like she was in another world.

"No baby, Momma is just fine," she responded, and went back to cooking and singing.

I sat down at the kitchen table, and watched Momma prepare a beautiful meal for Daddy.

"Does your head hurt?"

"I don't feel a thing," Momma insisted as she seasoned Daddy's plate of food with something from a strange can. She gave the potatoes another good stirring, and went to deliver Daddy his tray of food.

I was pretty hungry too, so I went to the stove, and raised the lid on the large pot.

"Get away from that stove," Momma said as she came back into the kitchen.

"Did you eat anything?" she said with great concern.

"No Momma I didn't," I said confused by the panic in her voice.

"Did you touch anything on this counter?" she questioned.

"No Momma, I just looked in the pot, I promise."

"Alright baby, go tell everybody that dinner is ready."

After making sure Daddy was out cold, Momma joined us at the table. We were almost finished eating. She ate a few bites, but could not hold anything down. As we were leaving the table Momma asked Carla and I to stay.

"I really need your help girls," she said with great seriousness.

"What is it Momma?" Carla said.

"I'm tired baby, real tired," she said looking much older than her actual age of thirty-three. "How would you guys feel about leaving?"

"Oh Momma, do you mean it. Could we really leave?" I asked having thought of this moment a hundred times.

"Where would we go?" Carla asked.

"I don't know all that yet, but I know I can't take this another minute."

"Daddy will be mad," Carla said.

"Let me worry about your Father. You and Sharon are the oldest and I need you to be big girls for Momma. I need you to pack some clothes and shoes in those old suitcases in the closet for all the children."

"What if Daddy wakes up?" I said. "He will beat us to death for trying to leave."

"Just do what I said," she ordered with more confidence than I had ever seen her have, when it came to Daddy.

Carla and I scrambled around the room both, scared that we would wake up the monster, and happy that we were leaving. Momma, however, strolled around the house preparing for our leave like there wasn't a very mean man, who had just set her hair on fire, in the next room. *Momma has gone crazy. Daddy finally pushed her over the edge.* Just then I became frightened. Who would take care of us when she went to the crazy house?

"Is everything ready?"

"Yes Momma," we said.

"Carla round up the children and Sharon, you get the baby," Momma commanded.

As we left out the back door, Momma went back in the house.

"Where are you going?" I asked.

"Just stay here," she said.

Momma was only gone for a minute, but to me it seemed like hours. When she emerged from the house she had some money clinched in her fists. We started up the street on foot. Our destination was unknown.

Chapter 6

Glenwood Battered Women's Shelter was a simple establishment, with strict rules and curfews. However, it was ten times better than living with Daddy. The police officer Momma flagged down after we had walked for some time had brought us here. We were given two rooms. The boys and Momma shared one and Carla, Mya, and I shared the other. The rooms consisted of two twin beds, a small black and white television, and a dresser with mirror. We had set times for meals, and set times that everyone had to be in their rooms at night. The girls and I would pretend we were adults with our own apartment. Momma even looked happy sometimes. She never spoke about Daddy, so we did not bring him up. Besides we were having too much fun. We were only able to bring a few things with us, so the people at the shelter gave us a voucher for new clothes. Our excitement was plentiful. It was non-existent for us to get clothes brand new from the store. We got really excited about our shopping trip. Momma even got money to get her an outfit and a wig. She needed it, because she had three interviews on Monday. The last time she worked was right before I was born, because Daddy would not let her have a job in peace. If he would get mad about something, he would come on her job, and show out. She would either get fired or be too ashamed to return.

"Stop running around this store," Momma said trying to grab Kerry who was starting to walk really well to be only 8 months old. 'Must be getting out of the way for another' the lady at the shelter said the day before. I don't think Momma thought that was funny.

"I can't decide on a dress, I like all of them," Carla said as she danced around with the new clothes pressed against her body.

"You have to choose one dress, a skirt and shirt, and a pair of shoes and hurry up! These children are driving me crazy. They act like they have never been to a clothing store before," Momma said getting frustrated.

"Well, it is our first time Momma," I said laughing, as I gathered up the children.

****

Our first weekend had gone well. The boys made friends with a little boy in the shelter named John. His fourteen year-old brother, Nathan, came to Momma's room, and gave them a haircut. They looked really handsome Monday morning for school. The lady in the room next to ours offered to press out our kinky hair. We were really grateful. I felt really welcome there.

"I am so proud of all of you," Momma said giving all of us a quick inspection.

"Momma you look prewty," Jason said through his missing teeth.

"Thank you baby. Wish me luck. I need to get a job today," Momma said kissing all of us good bye, and grabbing Kerry to drop him at the daycare.

As we waited for the bus I started feeling sick. Even though I was only in the sixth grade, I had already been to seven different schools. I was not looking forward to this again. Being the new kid at a school, with hand me down clothes and a nappy head was an invitation for trouble. Kids were really cruel. They don't realize how their teasing affects a person. You always get picked last in gym, and no one wants you to sit with them at lunch. It is very difficult to adjust.

"You think you're cute," Carla told Mya.

"I know I'm cute," Mya said, swinging her freshly pressed hair.

"We all look good," Carlos Jr. said, doing a Micheal Jackson dance he saw on the music video channel at the shelter. Daddy would have never let us watch worldly stuff.

I had forgotten about our new look just that quickly. Our clothes were not second hand. Our hair was not nappy. From the outside we looked like normal kids. No one would ever know that we came to the bus stop from the Battered Women's Shelter around the corner.

Carla's bus came first. She was in Jr. High now and went to a different school.

"Bye Carla," Jason said.

"Bye, be good. See yall after school," Carla said.

Our bus came right behind Carla's. We boarded the bus, and quickly found seats near the front. The ride was short, about five minutes, and the kids actually spoke to us.

"What school did you come from?" a little girl with braces on her teeth asked me.

"We moved here from California," I said making up a new life to go with my new look.

"Have you ever seen any famous people?" she asked very excited.

"Why yes, we lived near George Jefferson and Fred Sanford," I said continuing my lie.

"Wow, why did you guys move here?" she asked.

"My Daddy is a Captain in the Military, and he got transferred here," I said shamelessly while Mya and the boys were bursting with laughter behind me.

I went on and on until we pulled into the school. The little girl told me her name was Stephanie, and that she wanted to sit with me on the way home from school. *I am in a new place and I can be whatever I want to be.*

As we entered the school, we made a familiar trip to the office to get our class assignment. Momma had came on Friday morning to do the transfer. They would not have our school records that quick, so they would put us in whatever class had space, until they knew where to put us. The school would not know that I was in gifted classes, or that Carlos Jr. was in Reading Lab. This is what always happened, when we changed schools. We got our assignments, and went our separate ways. I played the part of a military brat all day. The cutest guy in my class actually talked to me. Life was good. I sat with Stephanie during lunch, and also on the ride home from school.

"How was your first day of school?" Momma asked as we entered the shelter's lounge area.

"It was great and I made a friend," I squealed.

"My teacher is from Africa," Mya announced.

"They got some good food," Carlos Jr. said rubbing his stomach.

Everyone was talking at once. We were all so happy.

"You can sing together, but you can't all talk together," Momma said overwhelmed with all the chatter.

"Did you get the job?" Carla asked.

"I don't know yet, they said they would call me. In the meantime, I am going to call my sister, and get her to loan me some money," she continued.

For the first time, I thought about home. We were forty miles away from Winston, in an even smaller town, called Lenoah. No one knew where we were. It was like; we dropped off the face of the earth. Momma was going to call Aunt Jean, to let her know that we were fine, and to get her to send some money. The little money she had snatched from Daddy's wallet was disappearing quickly. I think it was beginning to sink in, that she was alone in the world with six children. Something she had not thought about that Wednesday evening, when we left.

"Sharon where are you? We have been worried sick," Aunt Jean yelled.

"Jean it got real bad. I had to leave. I didn't have time to think, much less call anyone," Momma exclaimed.

"Where are you?" she asked again.

"At a Battered Women's Shelter," Momma muttered.

"At a what? Why are you there? What happened?" Aunt Jean shouted.

"Carlos has been beating on me for a long time. I tried to make my marriage work. Jean, I could not take it anymore. I'm tired of him beating on the kids. He has a baby on the way by Bernice, our church secretary, and when I confronted him about it, he jumped on me and set my hair on fire," Momma blurted out before bursting into tears.

"Why didn't you ever say anything?" Aunt Jean asked.

"I was ashamed. Carlos is a preacher. I thought that no one would believe me," Momma managed to get out between sobs. "After he beat me, and burned my hair, I just went blank. When I found the opportunity, I grabbed the kids and left."

"Is the shelter here in town," questioned Aunt Jean.

"No, we are in Lenoah, about thirty to forty-five minutes from Winston. I only have a little money left, and I don't have a job yet. Can you send me some money?"

"What are you going to do with six kids and no money? Does Ma know about this?" Aunt Jean asked.

"No! You are the only person that knows where I am. I had some interviews today. We will manage. Are you able to send some money?"

"I can send you about fifty dollars. That is all I have. You want me to ask Ma?"

"Oh No! Ma would never understand. She never liked Carlos anyway. I can't deal with the 'I told you so' speech right now. Fifty dollars will be fine for now. I should hear from one of those jobs soon."

"I will send it Western Union," Aunt Jean said.

"Thanks Jean. I love you, and please don't tell anyone," Momma pleaded.

"I won't," Aunt Jean promised.

After school the next day, Momma was real happy. She was dancing around the room with Kerry in her arms. She had a big smile on her face, which I had not seen in a long time.

"What's going on?" Carla asked.

"I got a job Carla. It is a good job. I will be sewing in a factory. I took a sewing test, and passed with flying colors," Momma exclaimed.

"When do you start?" I asked.

"On Monday. I am going to take the rest of the week, and try to find us a place to stay. The shelter will pay the first months rent, and the security deposit.

"Can I have my own room?" Carlos Jr. asked.

"Me too Momma," Jason said.

"I don't know about your own room, but I will try to get you your own bed. How about that?" Momma offered.

"Sounds good," the boys said.

"Now, I have to walk over to the shopping plaza, to get the money Jean sent. Who wants to go?

We all ran towards Momma at once, almost causing her to drop Kerry. We loved going to the store.

The shopping plaza was about a five-minute walk. We all held hands, and sang all the way there.

The lady behind the counter at the store, looked at us real strange. I never thought about it, but I guess Momma looked crazy with an arm baby, and five other kids all under the age of thirteen. People called us 'stair step children', whatever that meant. Although she was not a wild woman, with several different fathers for her children, the outside world apparently make their own assumptions. Momma counted out her money, adjusted Kerry on her hip, and proudly exited the store.

Back at the shelter it was Momma's night to cook. All the women had to share in the chores. As she prepared the meal, we set the table in the dining hall. Compared to our tiny two-bedroom house, the shelter was a mansion. It had an oversized kitchen, a dining hall, and a lounge with a ping-pong table and a wide screen television. The bathroom was in the hallway, and had a row of showers, sinks, and toilets. The boys had a smaller one, on the other end of the building. No males over seventeen were allowed in the shelter, so it was more females than males. To get inside the shelter you had to ring a loud doorbell. Sometimes the women's husbands would try to come and start trouble, so the security was tight.

"Dinner's ready," Momma yelled from the kitchen.

As we ran to the dining hall, we heard the deafening tones of the doorbell. It was after hours, so it took a while for the director to get the door. *Ding Dong. Ding Dong.* The sound drowned out the television, and the noisy children.

"Sharon," the director called.

"Yes," Momma said, as she came into the hallway.

"You have a guest. It is after hours, but she said she came a long way," the director said.

Looking puzzled, Momma slowly went to the door. Carla and I stood in some chairs, and peeked out the window.

"Jean," Momma gasped. "What are you doing here?"

"I wanted to make sure you were alright. Are they treating you good in here?" she said, trying to look around Momma into the foyer of the shelter.

"We are fine. Thank you for the money. We were just about to have dinner. Do you want to come in and see the kids?"

"No, I can't come in," she said as she kept looking around. "We need to talk. I don't think you thought about this. Carlos is a good man," Jean said. Her whole facial expression had changed. We leaned further out the window, so we could hear better.

"What are you talking about Jean? Look at my hair," Momma said as she snatched off her wig in disgust.

"Carlos came over to my house," Jean said.

"When," Momma demanded looking shocked.

"This morning, Sharon. He was really sick, and had been in the hospital. The man said he almost died."

"I must not have used enough ant killer," Momma mumbled.

"What did you say Sharon?" Jean questioned.

"Nothing, Jean. Listen, I'm not going back. Things are hard right now, but I just got a job, and we are going to make it," Momma said, a little less confident than before she came to the door.

"He really loves you, and he's sorry. He is taking some counseling classes."

"Why are you on his side? He beat me repeatedly, and the children. That is not right, especially for a preacher," Momma shouted.

"I am not taking sides. I just think the two of you should sit down and talk. He misses his kids. Carlos is their father. You can't keep them from him," Aunt Jean went on.

Stay strong Momma. We can't go back. Please Momma. Please. I sat in the window, with tears welling up in my eyes. I could not believe Aunt Jean.

"Carlos sat over my house for eight hours straight, talking about you and the kids," Jean said. "He was really upset and crying."

"I am not ready to talk to him yet," Momma said, unsure of her next move.

"I know he has messed up in the past, but don't throw your marriage away," Aunt Jean said. "I am your only sister, and Carlos knows that. I told him I did not know where you were, and he did not believe me. He would not leave my house."

Momma had to chuckle, thinking of Daddy ranting and raving for eight hours, practically holding Jean and Maurice hostage. "How did you get him to leave?"

I noticed that Momma was smiling, but Aunt Jean had a serious look on her face. Just then, I saw two men coming from the back parking lot. As they got closer to the front porch, I saw it was Daddy and Uncle Maurice.

"Jean, How could you? You promised!"

"Just talk to him," Jean said. "I did not know what else to do. He was so pitiful, and he would not leave."

"I can't believe you Jean. I trusted you," Momma cried.

"Hi Sharon," Daddy said as he kissed her tear-streaked cheeks. Momma jerked away, and tried to come inside. Daddy grabbed her arm with firm gentleness.

"Let's just talk. I'm sorry, and I love you," he proclaimed loudly. "I know you put something in my food, but I still love you," he growled softly in her ear, once he had pulled her back towards him.

"I'm not going back Carlos. You need help," Momma said. "You are supposed to be a man of God."

"I am getting some help. The VA hospital has a new counseling class. I called them up, and made an appointment. Things will be different," Daddy promised.

"What about Bernice and the baby?" Momma asked.

"Sharon I made a mistake. I can't change that, but I will resign from the church, and get a job," Daddy said.

"Carlos I don't know. The kids are finally happy, and they have started school."

"Those are my kids. God gave me those kids." Daddy said starting to get fired up. "If you want to stay here, fine, but my children are coming with me."

Momma started to cry uncontrollably. It was a blow to find out Daddy was alive, and a complete let down to know that he now knew where she was. She always said that leaving us with Daddy would never happen. *Thank God for that*. However, Momma also knew that he would not give her any peace, and definitely would find out where her new job was. He would be a constant thorn in her side. How could Aunt Jean and Uncle Maurice do that to Momma? They did not know Daddy like we did. No one knew what went on behind the pulpit.

"Sharon is everything o.k.?" the director asked. She had heard a man's voice, and came back to the door.

"Sir, I am going to have to ask you to leave. Men are not allowed on the premises."

"My wife and kids are on your so-called premises Lady," Daddy said in a very familiar tone. He was definitely about to act a fool.

"I am just going to get my things, Director Smith," Momma said between her sobbing.

"You don't have to go, Sharon. I can have them removed," she said.

"You don't understand my husband. He knows where I am now. There is no way I can stay here. Thank you for everything. I really appreciate it."

69

As Momma instructed us to get our things together, my heart sank. I could not believe we were going back. Everyone was crying, except Kerry. I was so hurt. It was like I had been Cinderella, and now the clock had just struck midnight. We had been teased with a normal life, for 6 whole days. As I carefully packed my new shoes, I wished that I could click them together, and go somewhere far away. Each step I took down the walkway was hard. My feet felt so heavy, like I could hardly lift them. Each step is literally embedded in my memory.

"God gave yall to me. No one can take you away," Daddy preached.

"Hi kids," Aunt Jean said helping us with our bags. "Who wants McDonalds?"

"I do. I do," Jason said.

"Shut up! We're supposed to be mad," Carlos Jr. said as he elbowed him in the ribs.

"I can't help it, I'm hungry," Jason said.

None of us had eaten any of the food Momma had just prepared. We had all been glued to the window, listening to what was going on outside. I don't know how we all were able to fit in Aunt Jean's car. Four adults, five kids, and one baby in a Buick. We looked like one of those cars, at the circus, with all the clowns in it. The worst part was that all the way home, Daddy preached and Momma cried. That is probably why Aunt Jean skipped McDonalds, and took us straight home.

Chapter 7

Daddy had kept his word about leaving First Prayer Church of God, but he did not resign. The controversy over Bernice's baby caused such a stink, that the members put him out. We moved to a three-bedroom house, about ten minutes west of Winston, and Daddy got a job at Reynolds. Even though we were not far from Winston, we never saw or heard from Bernice again. I later heard she moved back to her hometown, just before the baby was born.

The new house was nice. The girls shared a bedroom, and the boys shared one. Our room had a bunk bed set and a twin bed. The boy's room had a bunk bed set and a crib. We lived a pretty normal life in our new neighborhood. Daddy kept his appointment with the VA hospital. Momma got a sewing job at Indera Mills, and was able to buy a car. It was a station wagon, and we loved it. The payment was affordable, with both of them working.

"Today is Friday," Daddy called out from the doorway.

We all ran towards him. Every Friday he would get paid, and we would each get a dollar to go to the store. Dollar Fridays is the best memory I have of Daddy.

"I would like 25 pieces of penny candy, 25 strawberry penny cookies, and a sour pickle," Carla told Mrs. Herron at the store.

"Me too, Me too," we all echoed.

The store was next door to our new house. After leaving the store, we would sit on the front porch, and sing songs with Daddy. He actually seemed to be in a good mood. I think the therapy was helping.

Momma was enjoying the good times, but she had known Daddy since she was twelve. She knew that he could blow up at any moment. Her job had a credit union, and she took advantage of it, and opened a savings account, and began to secretly deposit money into it.

We joined a new church called Mt. Holy Church of God, near our house. It was much larger than the old one. The church was lively, and we thoroughly enjoyed it. Momma, Carla, Mya, and I all started singing on the choir. Daddy quickly made himself at home on the pulpit. After only a month of membership, he was named the Assistant Pastor. The technique Daddy had of having his sermons rhyme, along with his wild shouting, caught on even quicker. He became very popular in this new town.

"In Jesus name, it's still the same. One foot in front of the other, we'll go a little further," Daddy would shout from the pulpit.

Even Momma would stand up, and back him up. "Preach Elder Porter," she would say.

The one thing that really caused me grief about our return was that I had to go back to Kernersville Elementary School, after having left abruptly. Only to go there for two weeks, then move to the new house, and begin class at the ninth elementary school in my educational career. The moving around was taking a toll on my grades. Next school year I would be in Jr. High. I hoped I could get through those years at one school.

Chapter 8

"Girls hurry up," Daddy yelled as we scurried to get dressed. Momma was working overtime, and we were all going to spend the day at Grandma and Ronald's house. Daddy had some witnessing to do. On Saturdays he would stand in front of the Food Lion grocery store on M.L.K. JR Drive, and witness to people about Jesus Christ. He would also have an old Chitlin bucket with him, and take up donations for the church.

"Carla, get them children ready, and come on," Daddy said louder.

"Coming," she said.

The ride to Grandma's house required us to get on I-40, and go West for about fifteen miles. We had traveled about four exits, when Daddy began to slow down the old

Cadillac. He put on his right signal, and pulled over to the side of the road. Mya and Carlos Jr. had been pushing and shoving in the backseat. Daddy does not tolerate that, so I just knew somebody was going to get it.

"I told you to stop," Mya whispered and pushed Carlos Jr. again.

Scared to say anything out loud, but not about to let Mya get the last hit, Carlos shoved Mya without returning a word. Meanwhile, Daddy got out, and headed towards the front of the car.

"Mya, yall gon' get it," Jason said.

"But he's coming on your side of the car, Jason," Mya said.

"Shut up Mya, he's probably going to them bushes over there, to get a switch," I said. Daddy loved the extension cord, but if it were not around he would find a bush, and get three switches, and braid them together. He had a way of removing all the leaves with one swoop.

"Who are you telling to shut up. He might have seen you sucking your lip a minute ago. You know he don't like it when you do that."

We were all wrong. Daddy walked a ways in front of the car, towards a middle aged black man, who was on the side of the highway. He had a backpack, and was holding out his thumb. Daddy said a few words to him, and the both of them came back, towards the car.

"Daddy picking up another hitchhiker," Carla said.

"I am glad I'm in the front seat," I said. "I don't like sitting next to strangers."

"I know. I'm always scared when they are in the car," Carlos Jr. said.

"At least yall ain't getting no whipping, Carlos," Jason said.

Daddy always gave hitchhikers rides. They would get in the backseat, and get dropped off, at or close to their destination. He would do it when we traveled out of state as well. None of the men ever tried anything, but it always made me feel uncomfortable.

"Slide over and make room," Daddy said. "I am giving Mr…

"Onagangi, Babatunde Onagangi," the man said with an accent.

"I'm giving Mr. Onabangi a ride into town," Daddy replied not quite pronouncing the name right.

We rode into town in silence. I don't know what was on Daddy's mind sometimes.

We dropped the man off about a block from Grandma's house. Daddy shook his hand, and continued up Mt. Vernon Road. Ronald was in the yard when we pulled up. Their house was small, with two bedrooms and one bathroom. There was always something going on at Grandma's house. Aunt Brenda and her family lived there in one bedroom, and Uncle Timothy had a twin bed set up in the pantry. Ronald and Grandma's room was in the front of the house. They had a house full, not to mention the numerous dogs and cats running around.

"Hey," Ronald yelled from the chicken coop.

"Hi Ronald," we all replied.

"Mind your manners," Daddy said, as he sped away without speaking to Ronald.

All the kids ran in the house to see Grandma, but I stood frozen in one place. While waving to Ronald, I was taken aback by what he was doing. He was running around trying to catch one of the chickens. In a matter of moments, he had one in his hand. Carefully he slid his big hands around the chicken's neck, and began to swing it around. He did this continuously, over and over again. All of a sudden, the chicken separated in two. Ronald had the head in his hand, but the body fell to the ground. I was in total shock. The body danced around the mostly dirt front yard, seemingly unaware that his head was missing. I had never seen anything like that in my life. It brought new meaning to the saying 'like a chicken with his head cut off'.

"What are you staring at child?" Ronald asked, after becoming aware of my presence.

"Nothing," I stuttered, and ran up the walkway to the house.

Everyone was in Aunt Brenda's room. It was the largest one in the house. The one and only bathroom was also in this bedroom. It was furnished with one queen size bed, and a set of bunkbeds. There was also an oak entertainment center, with a large television. Rayna and Tasha were watching a movie, and we all spread out on the floor, to catch the ending.

After the movie, I went into the dining room to talk to Grandma. She was in her favorite chair, at her old wood table. As I entered the room, one of the dogs ran up to me. I am very scared of dogs, but I had to pretend that I wasn't, because Ronald gets real mad if you act afraid or scream. I held my breath, and waited for the dog to go away.

"Grandma do you have any candy?"

"Get my pocketbook baby," she said, pointing to her bedroom, with the knife she was cutting potatoes with.

I ran to her room, and tripped over an aluminum pan in the floor. The cloudy water in the pan spilled onto the floor, and a bar of soap slid across the room. Grandma used the pan to bathe. Although they had a bathtub, she always washed in her bedroom, in the pan. I quickly found a towel, got the water up, and ran back to the dining room.

"Here's your pocketbook," I said, without mentioning the spill.

As she fumbled through her purse, I noticed something black moving in the freshly cut potatoes.

"Grandma there is something crawling in the bowl," I shrieked.

"That ain't nothing but black pepper," she shot back, as she thumped the baby roach away from the bowl.

"Here's some candy baby," she offered me, and a couple of the other kids, that had gathered at the table.

"Tasha, who is that coming in the door?" Aunt Brenda asked from her bedroom, when she heard the screen door slam.

"It's Aunt Genene," Tasha replied.

Oh Lord. Here we go. The only time those two were not fighting, was when they were gossiping about somebody else. Either way, I knew things were about to get interesting. Aunt Genene did not even say hello, before she started running her mouth.

"Ma, Carlos down at the grocery store, acting a fool," she announced. "He is preaching at the top of his lungs. Just screaming, and carrying on like a mad man."

"Lord, he is going to end up in jail again for disturbing the peace," Grandma said.

"Ronald need to go get him," Aunt Brenda said, going to the front door, and calling for him.

When he did not answer, she went around to the back door, and called out to him again.

"Just a minute, Brenda," he yelled, from the side of the house.

Before he had a chance to come inside, Daddy had pulled up, and stormed in the house.

"The manager told me that he does not want you in front of his store anymore," Aunt Genene said, immediately starting in on Daddy.

"I knew you was going to fly over here, to run your big mouth," Daddy yelled.

"Don't start," Grandma said. "I don't want to hear it."

"Then tell your son to stop acting crazy all the time. That is very embarrassing," Aunt Genene said.

As if the mention of the word crazy was lighter fluid, Daddy went off.

"Carla, get the children, and get in the car," Daddy commanded, as he called Aunt Genene a witch and a troublemaker. Happy to be leaving, we all rushed to the door.

"Yall not going to stay for dinner?" Ronald asked, coming up the front steps holding the chicken I saw him kill earlier.

"No Ronald we got to go," I said about to throw up thinking about that chicken.

Daddy shot past Ronald without a word, and we sped off in the old Cadillac.

Chapter 9

Daddy was usually gone to work before we got up for school. This morning he was sitting at the kitchen table.

"What are you doing here Daddy?" Jason asked.

"Don't I live here boy?" he said.

"Yes sir," Jason replied and quickly left the room.

Hearing Daddy's voice made Momma come into the kitchen.

"Carlos, what are you doing here?"

"Look, this is my house, and I will not be questioned," he yelled, as he slammed his fist down on the table.

When we left the house to go to the bus stop, I could still hear Daddy screaming. *Oh no, not again!* Daddy had been on his best behavior, since we had been back. *Lord; please don't let him snap!*

Thoughts of my parents ran through my mind all day. I wondered if Daddy had calmed down, and let Momma go to work. All day my concentration was off. I thought about her, and Kerry being trapped in the house, and Daddy hurting them.

"Times up everyone. Make sure your name is on your test, and pass them up." Mr. Ebrom said.

Just then I looked down at my test, and it was completely blank. I had only put my name and the date on the paper. Quickly, I folded the test in two, and put it inside my desk. Mr. Ebrom would have to figure out where my test was. Maybe he would think it had gotten misplaced, and let me retake it.

When the final bell rang, I could not wait to get home. I was worried about Momma. Daddy had missed his last therapy session at the VA hospital, and that was not good. When we got home, Daddy's Cadillac was flying up the hill away from the house. I did not see Momma or her car, and I breathed a sigh of relief. *Daddy must have calmed down.*

Momma came in the door a short while later, with Kerry and a bag of groceries. I ran to her, and hugged her real tight.

"You were on my mind all day. I thought Daddy's metal plate had moved again."

"I am fine," Momma said. "Your Daddy was upset because he lost his job. He was trying to boss his supervisor. He also got a second denial from the VA, for some benefits he felt he deserved."

"Did he hit you Momma?" Mya asked, as all the other kids came in the kitchen.

"He promised he wouldn't! He promised," Carlos Jr. shrieked.

"No baby, there was no hitting. He just went on and on for about an hour, and made me late for work."

"Did you get in trouble?" Carla asked, knowing that Momma had been late several times for different reasons.

"I got another point on my attendance record, but I'm going to hold on as long as I can."

As we sat at the kitchen table and did our homework, Momma began to prepare dinner. She had escaped a beating, but for how long. Daddy was definitely headed down a familiar path. When dinner was ready, Daddy was not home yet, so we gladly ate without him.

Thursday night we always gathered around the television to watch The Cosby Show, and this night was no exception. We all settled in front of the tube, waiting to see what crazy predicament Rudy and Vanessa would get into. The show had only been on for two minutes, when it was interrupted for a special announcement from the President of the United States.

"I hate the president," I said frustrated with the intrusion.

"What did you say young lady?"

I had no idea that Daddy had come home. Everyone froze up, and the room was dead silent.

"You don't ever say you hate anybody. Where did you get that kind of talk from?"

I could not speak. All the other kids sat motionless on the floor. Terror was in everyone's eyes, especially mine. Whatever the president said, went unheard by everyone in the room.

"I am going to beat your butt. Get in the kitchen, and finish cleaning the table off for your Momma. When you finish, I am going to whip your tail!"

Slowly I made my way to the kitchen table, and began to wipe. Our table was square, and made out of wood. I wiped from corner to corner, with small circular motions. When I reached the end of the table, I quickly started over. Knowing that once I finished, I was going to get thrashed by Daddy. Suddenly I had to use the bathroom, but I dared not stop, for fear of my upcoming beating. The wiping continued for over an hour. When I felt like my arm was about to fall off, I happened to look up, and there was Daddy standing in the doorway. The sudden adrenaline rush allowed me to continue my chore. The dishcloth was not even wet anymore, but I wiped, wiped, wiped. I did not look back up from the table. The next thing I heard, was uncontrollable laughter. My Daddy was in the doorway, laughing hysterically at me. I was scared to death, and this man was laughing at me. Daddy left the room, and I continued. A long while later Momma came in, and told me to go to bed.

"What about Daddy?" I asked.

"Child, he has been asleep for over thirty minutes. I did not know you were still in here. Go to bed," she said.

Tears began to flow freely down my face, as I ran to my bedroom. That was so cruel of him. I know I said something bad about the president, but I did not mean it. The Cosby Show was my favorite. I wished Cliff Huxtable was my Daddy. He was always nice to his children, I thought, as I fell into an exhaustion-induced sleep.

****

Since Daddy no longer had a job, he threw himself into the church even more. He was always away, doing something for the Lord. His latest project was teaching all the ladies in the church to drive. He would take them to empty parking lots and deserted parks to do his training. Everyone at Mt. Holy loved Elder Porter, and women in their thirties and forties, who had never driven before, wanted lessons.

Momma's cousin went to our church, and she also wanted to learn to drive. Her name was Nancy, and the night before her lesson, she spent the night with us. At eighteen years old, she was six years older than Carla was. Her long hair was really pretty. We were all ready for bed, when Daddy came in the room that night.

"Nancy, I put out a pillow and blanket for you in the living room," Daddy said.

Even though we had already worked out the sleeping arrangements in our room, we dared not override what Daddy said.

"Good night Nancy," we said as she left the room.

"Good night," she responded.

We rarely had overnight guests, and were thoroughly enjoying her company. Mya and I had taken the top bunk, and given Nancy the bottom. I did not feel like climbing down right then, so I laid my head back and soon fell asleep.

Mya woke me up with a sharp kick in my side. It was the middle of the night, and I decided to get in my own bed. As I climbed down, I had a strong urge to use the bathroom.

I walked into the hallway without turning the light on, and bumped into Momma.

"You gotta pee too, Momma," I asked rubbing my eyes.

"Shhh, I heard something in the living room, and of course your Daddy is not here to protect us," Momma said, with a bat in her hand.

"Oh my goodness! You gotta hurry. Nancy is in the living room. Daddy made her leave our room, and sleep in there," I whispered. Forgetting I had to go to the bathroom, I crept behind Momma, towards the living room.

"What in the world?" Momma questioned, as she entered the living room.

"It is not what you think, Sharon," Daddy said.

When I peeked in the room, I saw Daddy and Nancy sitting on the couch with a blanket over them. Nancy had a blank look on her face, and he was trying to explain.

"I could not sleep, so Nancy and I were watching a movie," he said. "It was a little chilly in here, so we got under the blanket."

I guess he did not realize that the television station had signed off, and was making that high pitch sound. Momma made me and Nancy go back to my bedroom, and she and Daddy went at it.

"Are you o.k.?" I said to Nancy, after using the bathroom, and joining her in my bedroom.

"I feel sick," is all she said, before climbing in my bed, and getting into a fetal position. In a matter of minutes, she was asleep. I debated on whether to get in my bed with Nancy, or climb back up with Mya. On the floor, by the door, is where I ended up. Things were really heated up in the living room.

"You nasty, dirty dog. You have no respect for me, your kids, or the church."

"Sharon, I am the head of this house, and I will not let you take that tone with me. I explained to you what was going on."

"You must think I am stupid. What are you going to do, when she tells someone at the church what happened?"

"There's nothing to tell."

"I'm so tired of you and your mess. I should have never come back. You are never going to change."

"What do you mean 'you should have never come back'. Who do you think you are?"

Daddy must have hit Momma, because I heard her scream. Next there was a lot of crashing sounds, and more screaming. I listened to the loud noises and preaching, until I fell asleep. It had only taken three months, for his old ways to fully resurface.

Chapter 10

Momma's poor attendance record made her eventually lose her job. Daddy was back to beating her on a regular basis. Even though his record was long, he never got any real time in jail when the police would come.

Life got pretty hard with no one working. Daddy got a salary from the church, but he gave most of it back in the offerings. Momma quickly depleted the money she had been saving.

"Momma the water won't work," Carlos Jr. said one morning. Today was July the 20th 1987, his ninth birthday. Momma had given him his one and only birthday present. It was a multi colored 2-piece short outfit, which she had made. He was excited to bathe, and put his new outfit on.

"Let me try," Mya said, coming into the bathroom.

Sure enough, nothing came out of the faucet. Momma looked so disgusted. Daddy had not been there when she woke up, and she did not know where he was. We would probably miss another day of school.

Momma gathered all the empty jugs and containers she could find, and we went to Ronald's house to fill them up with water. This was the second time we had had to do this, and it was very embarrassing. We would bring the water home, and warm it on the stove, to take a bath or wash the dishes. Sometimes we would have to reuse the water.

"Momma, can we get water from somewhere else?" I asked.

"Why you ask, baby?" Momma said.

"They laughed at us the last time," Carla said.

"Who?" Momma questioned.

"While we were filling the jugs, Aunt Brenda called Aunt Genene on the phone, and they were laughing," I said.

"Don't worry about them," Momma said. "Brenda doesn't even have her own house."

The whole ride to Ronald's I prayed that no one would be there, except Grandma.

"Look Momma, Aunt Genene is here," Mya said, as we arrived at the house.

Actually, the entire driveway and street were filled with cars. Aunt Genene's, Aunt Brenda's, Uncle Timothy's, and some other cars I did not recognize. Daddy's old Cadillac was there, and Momma got out to find him, and see what was going on.

We had been in the car for a few minutes, and Kerry was thirsty and crying. Mya and I grabbed a couple of the jugs, and Carla got the baby. We all ran towards the house. When we got to the front door, all eyes were on us. There we were unbathed, and carrying empty jugs. We must have looked a mess. Everyone stopped what they were doing, and just stared at us. Momma motioned us back out the door, and we got in the car and left.

"We didn't get the water," Carlos Jr. said.

"I know baby, we'll figure out something."

"Why are all those people at Ronald's house?" I asked.

"Kids, your Uncle Bud has passed away," she said.

"What do you mean?" Jason asked. He was three months from being eight years old, and did not understand.

"Uncle Bud has gone to live with Jesus," Momma replied.

"Did he take all the candy with him?" Jason shrieked.

We all laughed at Jason, and Momma explained it to him as best as she could.

"What happened Momma?" I asked.

"It was the diabetes. He wasn't taking his medicine, or eating right. It finally got the best of him."

I was saddened by the news. Uncle Bud was my favorite uncle, and I would truly miss him.

As we pulled up to our house, Daddy was coming down the hill behind us. When he got out of the car, I could tell he had been crying. He was upset about his brother's death.

"Drink, I want drink," Kerry whined.

We were all pretty thirsty and dirty. A bath was calling all our names. The house was beginning to smell, from the waste build up in the toilet. With the water being off, we were unable to flush the toilet. Daddy was consumed with Uncle Bud's death, so Momma had to think of something all by herself. She could not call her Mother. Grandma would go off on her real bad, and she would not be able to handle that right now. Momma walked over to the store next door, and once again dialed Aunt Jean's number.

"Hey Jean, its Sharon."

"Hey sis, how's it going."

"Well, I gave it a try, and Carlos is back to beating on me. He tried to have sex with cousin Nancy, and our water is turned off for the second time," Momma said, without stopping to breathe.

"Sharon, I am really sorry. I feel so responsible."

"I know I never gave you that fifty dollars back, but I need some money to get the water back on. Ronald Jr. died today, and Carlos is no help right now."

"I'm sorry to hear about Bud. How much is the bill?" Aunt Jean said.

"Hold on Jean."

"What baby?" Momma said, in response to me tapping on her arm. I had been standing there, waiting for an opportunity to break in.

"Excuse me for interrupting, but we found this change in the car and in the couch. Can we get a big drink from the store, and share it? Kerry is thirsty and crying."

"Go ahead," Momma said, trying to hide her tears.

"I'm back. The total bill is one hundred and seven dollars, but we can pay fifty-two dollars to have the service restored. Can you help me?"

"I feel so bad. I will give you the whole bill, but what are you going to do?"

"I don't know. I have no idea," Momma said. "Some days I feel like just disappearing, but I can't leave my kids. Our address is 12856 Thomasville Road. Can you pay it today? The bill is in my name."

"Sure, I will go now. I love you Sharon, and I am so sorry."

"Thank you, Jean."

Even though Aunt Jean paid the bill, they did not turn the water back on until the next day, which was Thursday. When we got up, we knew the water was on, because we heard Daddy taking a shower.

"Sorry something didn't even ask how I got the water back on."

"What did you say, Momma?" Mya asked, as we prepared for school.

"Nothing baby. Yall hurry up and get your baths, and have a good day at school."

****

Uncle Bud's funeral was the following Tuesday. Everything was chaotic, as normal with the Porter Family. Aunt Brenda was fussing about her name being misspelled in the obituary. Aunt Linda was there, and she was upset because Aunt Genene had left her name off altogether.

As we moved forward in a single file line to view the body, there was suddenly a loud crash. Uncle Timothy had been leaning over the casket crying, and knocked it over. Poor Uncle Bud ended up all twisted on the floor. The funeral directors quickly rushed to the front of the church, to fix the situation. They instructed the pallbearers to surround the casket, while they picked Uncle Bud up off the floor. The pallbearers made it difficult to see what was going on. Everybody was standing up, trying to catch a glimpse of Uncle Bud. When everything was back in order, the pastor quickly began the eulogy, without continuing the viewing of the body. Although Daddy did not preach the funeral, they were wise to give him a space at the end, or he would have taken it anyway.

"Let the church say, Amen," Daddy started, with his favorite opening.

"Amen," the church responded.

"My brothers and sisters in the Lord, we are gathered here today, to remember the life of Ronald Porter II. I would like to recite a poem for him. This poem is off the cuff. For those of you who don't know what that means, I'll tell you. It means that the words I say to you today have never made it on paper. A pen or pencil has never written these words. As it comes to my mind, so shall I speak."

Ronald II. was my brother.

He and I really love our Mother.

Now he is gone.

I won't cry or moan.

He had two kids.

Yes he did.

He is in a better place.

By Gods grace.

In Jesus name.

It's still the same.

One foot in front of the other.

We will go a little further.

Daddy ended with a song that was loud and long. Aunt Genene joined in with him. Whenever Daddy stopped singing, she would start the song back up. When she stopped, he would start it back up. They began to walk around the church, and shove the microphone in different people's face, for them to sing. It was a circus. The funeral was packed, and they were acting a fool.

Aunt Tangerine, Cousin Cheryl and Cousin Ronald III.
all sat motionless on the front row. As the circus continued,
they dared not say a word. Uncle Bud had always protected
his family from the Porter's craziness, but now he was gone.
Aunt Genene and Aunt Brenda had not waited until he was
in the ground, before they had barged into Aunt Tangerine's
home. They helped themselves to whatever they wanted.

They claimed that Uncle Bud would have wanted
them to have certain things. The kids were young and
Aunt Tangerine was too meek to stand up to them. She
occasionally had seizures, but was able to function just fine.
I could see the fear in her eyes at the funeral. New Jersey
was her hometown, but she had moved to North Carolina
with Uncle Bud a long time ago. She had no family in
Winston. Uncle Bud loved Tangerine and his kids, and
would turn over in his grave, once he made it there, if he
knew what was going on.

There was one person missing from the funeral. It
was Ronald Sr. He had gotten dressed in his one good suit,
and drove to the church. However, for reasons unknown to

me, he did not come inside. I thought that was weird. Then again the entire Porter family was acting crazy that day.

Chapter 11

"Sharon, get back in here," Daddy yelled from the kitchen.

I slowly reentered the room, trying to think of what I had done wrong.

"I know you are not still sucking your lip. Your teeth already stick out. What are you trying to do?"

"I'm sorry Daddy. I just can't help it." I had been sucking my lip for as long as I can remember.

"I told you I did not want you sucking your lip," he yelled. "You are hard headed, but I am going to fix you."

I started crying just thinking of what Daddy was going to do to me. I was either going to get a beating, stand in the corner on one leg, or kneel on rice. Either way I would be in pain.

"Daddy, I really try to stop. Sometimes I don't even know that I am doing it," I pleaded.

No response came from him; he just busied himself with a small cardboard box that he had on the table.

"Come here, Sharon." I reluctantly came closer.

"Open your mouth," he shouted. Looking puzzled, I just stood there.

"I said open your mouth," he said, as he grabbed my jaws, and forced a square shaped piece of cardboard in between my lips.

"Keep this in your mouth, and I better not see you take it out. I am going to call your teacher, and tell her to let me know if you take it out at school today," he said.

Oh my God! Daddy has really lost his mind. How am I supposed to go to school like this? Daddy was just crazy enough to call my teacher, so I tried to think of how I would get through the day. As we walked to the bus stop, I longed for the few days of happiness we had at the shelter.

"Hey bald head Sharon! Why you got paper in your mouth? Are you a goat or something?" I turned around to see Nicki Herron. Her Dad owned the store next door to our house. Daddy had wasted no time in informing all the kids at the bus stop of his rules regarding fighting for his children. As in the past, this caused us to be tormented by at least one or two kids. Nicki was a lot worse than Marsha was, though. She not only physically abused us, she launched a full verbal attack, anytime she felt like it. I wonder if she knew how much she would hurt my feelings.

"Look everybody, bald head Sharon has to eat paper, because they don't have no food," Nicki teased.

Uncontrollable laughter erupted at the bus stop, and I was furious. I wanted to respond and say something clever, but instead I just sat on the curb, and waited for the bus to come. Mya and the boys came over, and tried to console me.

"Don't worry about her," Carlos Jr. said.

"She is just jealous of your new dress Moma made," Mya said. I looked up at her and smiled. Although I knew Nicki was not the least bit jealous of me, I had to pull myself together for the younger kids. Carla was in Jr. High and I was the second oldest.

As the bus neared our stop, I stood up from the curb. Something did not feel right. My new dress felt wet. I pulled the back of my dress around to take a closer look. There, smack dead in the middle, was a large red stain. I suddenly felt sick to my stomach.

"Mya, something is wrong. I have to go back home, so take care of the boys today." Those were the first words I had said, since Daddy had shoved the cardboard in my mouth. I was so shaken by the sight of blood, I had nearly forgotten about it. As the words exited my mouth, so did the cardboard. It landed in the dirt. The wetness from my mouth, made the dirt stick to it like a magnet. I carefully waited until everyone had boarded the bus. When it began to pull off, I grabbed the cardboard and ran home. Not knowing if Daddy would believe what happened to it, I brushed it off and put it back in my mouth as I came through the door.

"Momma, look at my dress," I said trying to hold the paper in my mouth, and talk at the same time.

"Girl, what's in your mouth? I can't understand you."

"Daddy made me put this cardboard in my mouth, so I wouldn't suck my lip. Look at my dress, Momma!" I shrieked.

She looked really shocked at how far Daddy would go, and even more shocked at my dress.

"Take that paper out your mouth and come here."

"But Daddy," I began.

"I said take it out. That is ridiculous for him to do that to you," Momma yelled.

I looked around the room, waiting for Daddy to emerge and flip out.

"Who are you looking for? Your Daddy left right after you did," Momma said.

I had been in such a panic, that I did not even notice that the old Cadillac was gone.

"Why am I bleeding?" I asked as I breathed a sigh of relief.

"You got your cycle baby. You are becoming a woman."

"What does it mean? Why Carla ain't become a woman yet?" I blurted out.

"Different people start at different times. Your body is beginning to develop, and your cycle is one of the changes. You will have one every month, around the same time. Let's go to the bathroom, and I will show you what to do," Momma offered.

"Can I tell you something?" I said, as we entered the bathroom.

"Yes baby," she replied.

"I don't mean to be disrespectful, but Daddy is so mean to us. I wish we could go back to the shelter, because we were happy there. Weren't you happy there Momma?"

"Yes I was, but when Jean brought your Daddy there, I did not know what to do."

"Can we leave again. We could go really far this time, and not tell anyone where we are."

"Baby, I know it is hard for you to understand. I also know that things are getting back to the way they were, before we left. You have got to trust me. I'm going to get us out of this situation."

Momma gave me something called a napkin, and showed me how to position it. It was the thickest napkin I had ever seen, and it made me walk funny. I went into the living room, and joined Momma on the couch. We spent the rest of the day sewing.

Momma was a very good seamstress, and had begun to sew all the time now. When a holiday or birthday came around, she would make the girls a little doll or make the boys a cool hat.

People had started inquiring about some of the items she made. Momma soon began making things for other people, for money. The good thing was that she set her own prices, and Daddy could not keep up with the amount of money she made. This enabled her to put away a good amount for a rainy day. In addition to clothes and hats, she began to make fancy handkerchiefs, refrigerator magnets, and wall fans. When Xavier Roberts invented the Cabbage Patch Kids, we wanted one so bad. Of course we could not afford them, so Momma came to the rescue. Her doll had a soft body, and was just as good, in our eyes. She made each doll a unique outfit, and stitched whatever name we chose on the collar. Also each one came with a social security card, and a change of clothes. We were very proud of our dolls.

They soon began to cause a buzz in the community. Momma sold a lot of dolls, and landed herself in the newspaper. There was even a picture of her right above her new title. The caption read "The Doll Lady."

****

In between beatings and all night preaching sessions, Momma continued to sew and stash money, here and there. She would always tell Carla and I to hang in there. We trusted her, and on the hard days we thought about her secret plan for us to escape. We imagined a full scale Underground Railroad type of departure. The thought of leaving was the only saving grace we had. Today was one of those hard days. Jason and Carlos Jr. had been playing in the attic. The floor must have been weak, because as Mya and I did our homework, the boys came crashing down, into our bedroom. The fall left a large hole in our ceiling.

"Are you guys o.k.?" I asked, knowing that Daddy would be very mad.

"We were just playing," Jason said crying.

He was probably thinking the same thing that I was. As I turned to get Momma, Daddy was already in the doorway. I stepped backwards, into the corner, as he entered the room.

"We were just playing," Jason repeated. The words were almost inaudible through the tears.

Without asking any questions, Daddy summoned for Carla, who was the only one missing. When she entered the room, he announced that we were all getting a whipping.

"Get on your knees, and pull your pants down," Daddy commanded.

As he left the room, we all kneeled up against Carla's bed, and pulled our pants down. Pieces of sheetrock covered the floor, and pierced our knees.

"I'm going to get you for the old and the new," Daddy said, upon returning.

Daddy went down our row of bare butts with great intensity. Five licks for Carla, five licks for me, and so on. When he reached Jason at the end, he started over.

"Shut up! I don't want to hear anything," Daddy yelled, as he continuously swung the wooden stick at our

114

bottoms. I grabbed the sheets really tight, and tried not to scream, as the wood met my flesh and left a splinter behind. Poor Jason was only eight, and he could not hold back his screaming. Daddy began to beat him over and over again, telling him to shut up. He tried to stop screaming, but he couldn't. The more he screamed the more Daddy beat him. Then, as if nothing had happened, he left out of the room, and closed the door.

I slowly raised my head off the bed, and was horrified at what I saw. All our legs were bleeding and beginning to swell. Jason had a large gash on his butt, and you could see his white meat. He was still kneeling in the same position, as if he couldn't move.

"Are you alright."

Jason didn't move, or answer me. I held him, and even though I was only eleven, I tried to comfort him. Moments later, we heard the doorknob turning. Like soldiers we were all at attention.

"Momma," Carla screamed, knowing that Daddy must be gone for her to be at our door.

She came into the room crying, and 18-month-old Kerry was right behind her. I was glad that he was too little to get beat. Daddy always waited until each child was three years old, before he started giving it beatings.

"Oh my babies," she said, examining our wounds, and pulling out splinters.

"It hurt," Jason said, showing her his butt.

Momma began to cry uncontrollably.

"I'm so sorry kids. Things will get better, I promise. I know you can't understand right now, but please just trust me," she pleaded. When Momma had tended to everyone, she began to clean up the mess in the floor.

"How in the world did you all manage to come through the ceiling?" she asked.

"We were just playing," Jason said.

"Maybe the floor was weak," Carla said.

"I don't know what happened, but we have to get it fixed. The landlord will have a fit."

"Do we have to go to church tonight, my legs really hurt?" Mya asked.

"You trying to start your Daddy up again, young lady. I want you all to come and eat dinner, and then get ready for church," she responded.

The only beatings we missed church for were Momma's. I guess Daddy could justify beating us to the congregation, but not beating Momma. Everyone but Jason sat down to eat dinner. He wanted to stand, because the gash on his butt was sore. After dinner, we washed up and went to our rooms to get dressed. Momma picked out the longest dresses we had, and laid them on the bed. As I looked down at my legs, I began to cry again. They were discolored, and very sore. I could hardly pull my stockings up, without brushing against the open wounds.

"You need some help, Sharon?" Momma offered.

"It hurt so bad. I can't take it Momma," I said. "Why does Daddy hate us so much?"

"It's not that he hates us. He just does not know how to love us," Momma replied.

Just as Momma finished getting Kerry dressed, Daddy pulled up, and began to honk the horn. We all piled into the old Cadillac, and began our journey to an out of town church. Daddy had been invited there to be a guest speaker for a revival. It was about a thirty-minute ride, and we all fell asleep. I don't know how long I was sleep, but a rush of cold air suddenly awakened me.

"Oh no," I yelled.

Daddy was steadily driving down the highway, unaware that Mya, who was ten years old, had fallen out the door.

"Daddy, Mya fell out the car," I screamed.

By that time everyone was awake. While Daddy pulled over, we all watched in amazement, as Mya held on to the inner door handle in total silence. She did not make a sound. I think she was in shock. Daddy came around, and helped her back into the car. The front of her legs now matched the back of her legs, in terms of bruises. Everyone in the car was silent, including Mya. She never once cried, and just stared out the window.

Daddy led us into a long prayer, before driving off. He preached the rest of the way to the church. As we pulled up to the church, we knew what time it was. It was time to put on our happy faces, and pretend that we were the perfect family. Daddy proudly walked into the church, and took his seat behind the pulpit. We all found seats in the congregation. When it was his time to preach, he did his normal routine.

"Let the church say, Amen," Daddy commanded.

"Amen," the church responded.

"Giving honor to God, who is first in my life. I would also like to thank God for my beautiful family."

That was our cue to stand, smile and be recognized. Next Daddy would request that we sing a song, before he began his sermon.

We made our way to the front of the church, and stood side by side. The song we sang was already preselected by Daddy, on the way there. As Carla sang the lead, I thought about Mya falling out the car. I think she was trying to escape, and I don't blame her. We got a standing ovation for our song, and Daddy looked very pleased. When I glanced at him, all I could think was; *I hope Momma's secret plan kicks in soon, before Daddy kills us.*

Chapter 12

Every since Uncle Bud's death, Ronald had been spending a lot of time at Aunt Tangerine's house. He would make sure they were all right into the wee hours of the morning sometimes. I am sure Uncle Bud would appreciate Ronald looking out for his family. Cheryl and Ronald III. were having a hard time with their Daddy's death. Every time we saw them, they were always really quiet, especially Cheryl. Even Aunt Tangerine seemed different. Except for an occasional seizure, she had always been upbeat, but lately, her eyes seemed dark, and empty. She began to gain weight, and slip further into an unknown place. Ronald was always with them. I was glad someone was there, to make sure they were o.k.

Today, just like the last two times we had stopped by Aunt Tangerine's house, Ronald's car was there.

I don't know why, but as we got out of the car Daddy mumbled "dirty dog". Not knowing, who he was referring to, or what was on his mind, I quickly jumped out of the car, and got away from him.

"Hey Cheryl," I said, as I entered the living room.

"Hey," she stammered, after glancing at Ronald first, as if to get permission.

"Aunt Tangerine, can I have some candy, please?" Jason asked.

"I... I... don't... don't have any candy, baby," she stuttered.

Aunt Tangerine always had candy. They had a store. Something was very wrong with her.

"Hi Tan, how's it going," Momma said.

"Fine," was all she said in response, and she never raised her head.

The house seemed very cold, and I suddenly wanted to go outside.

"Let's go outside and play," I offered.

Everybody ran to the door, except for Cheryl and Ronald III. When we got outside, I noticed that they hadn't come, and I went back to the door.

"Can we go play Ronald?" I heard Cheryl ask, in a small voice.

Ronald peered at her, like she smelled bad. Then he looked at Ronald III. He was watching Jason and Carlos Jr. from the window.

"Get out of that window boy," Ronald snapped. "Gone outside."

I jumped back from the door as they came out, so Ronald would not see me. He must be in a bad mood. He probably needs some rest, since he's been trying to take care of two households. I decided that that was the reason he was crankier than normal. We played in the yard for a while, and everyone seemed to really have a good time. The front yard was mostly dirt, and made it perfect for kickball. It was two of them and five of us so the teams were not even. We decided to play the boys against the girls.

"It's time to go," Daddy yelled, before we were ready to leave. We were having fun, and wanted to continue. The second time we heard his voice, we knew to high tail it to the car. As I walked away, Cheryl grabbed my arm.

"Don't go. I mean, do you want to spend the night or something?"

"I wish I could, but you know Daddy won't allow us to spend the night no where," I responded.

Cheryl had an almost desperate look in her eyes, and she was still holding my arm.

"What's wrong with you?" Carla asked, when she saw Cheryl clinging on to me.

"I...I...," Cheryl struggled.

"What? What is it?" we asked.

"Cheryl," Ronald called from the door.

"I just miss my Daddy," she said, as she ran towards the house.

"Cheryl act like she slow," Mya said.

"Something is wrong with her and her Momma," I said.

"Some people deal with death in different ways," Carla said in her grown up voice. Every since she turned twelve, she thought she knew everything.

Daddy was already in the car honking the horn for us. As we ran to the car, I noticed Cheryl looking out her bedroom window. I waved to her, and she quickly moved away from the window. Neither Daddy nor Momma mentioned anything about the strange behavior of Uncle Bud's family. Daddy immediately started teaching us a song, he wrote for us to sing that night at church.

I just don't know. I just don't know.
Where I can go. Where I can go.
Without the Lord.

I just can't see. I just can't see.
Where I'd be. Where I'd be.
Without the Lord.

Daddy was singing and screaming at the top of his lungs.

"Sing with enthusiasm," he commanded.

I concentrated real hard on my part. He was real serious about our singing, because we always opened up for him. It seemed to make him very proud, when people praised him about our voices.

"Why aren't you singing, Sharon? We are going to do this song tonight," Daddy said to Momma.

"We need to *do* the bills."

"What did you say? Huh, what did you say?" Daddy shouted, as he repeatedly slammed his fist down on the dashboard.

"We need to take care of the bills, Carlos. Where's the money you got from the guest speakers offering the other night?" Momma said, in the most non-confrontational voice she could find.

It did not work. He went crazy. The car was weaving all over the road. Jason crouched down in the floorboard of the car, and covered his ears. He would always do this, when Daddy got mad in the car. He was very afraid of Daddy, and always trembled when he got loud.

"I work for the Lord. The Lord is my shepherd. I shall not want," he shouted, as he hit Momma really hard in her face. The powerful blow sent her head flying into the window. She was still, as if the window was holding her there. Even though Momma did not move, Daddy continued to yell and preach. His crazy driving had attracted the attention of a police officer, and we were being pulled over.

"Sit up Sharon," Daddy yelled, as he straightened his clothes, and glanced at us in the backseat.

"Don't say a word kids," he warned

When the policeman came up to the car, he calmly rolled the window down.

"What can I do for you today officer?"

"You changed lanes without signaling, a while back. License and registration please."

It had just begun to get dark, and the officer's partner shined his flashlight in the backseat, as Daddy fumbled for his registration. Jason was still in the floor, and silently crying. One by one the officer shined the light in each of our faces. *Shine it on my Momma! Please, shine it on my Momma!* I was scared, because she still had not moved. As if he heard my thoughts, he went around to the passenger side of the car. He tapped on the window with the flashlight.

"Ma'am are you all right?"

Momma slowly raised her head, and shielded her eyes from the bright light.

"Are you o.k.," the officer repeated.

Before she could answer, everybody's attention was redirected to Daddy, and the other officer. He had taken Daddy's info back to his squad car, and ran it through to the dispatcher.

"Mr. Porter, your license has been suspended for a failure to appear on a traffic ticket. They have issued a warrant, and I have to take you in."

"You better come and get me right away," Daddy said, as he leaned over to Momma and kissed her on the same cheek he had just hit. He suddenly found fifty dollars, and threw it in her lap. Daddy got out of the car, looked back, and gave Momma the look of death.

"That is *Elder* Porter, officer," Daddy said, as the policeman led him away.

After making sure they were long gone, I got out of the car, and helped Momma get in the driver's seat.

"Let's leave him in jail," Carla said.

"Baby, I wish I could, but his charge is very small. He will be out in no time, whether I go or not." Momma said, as she took off in the direction of the police station.

When we arrived at the police station, we all sat on an empty bench, and Momma went to the counter. As she talked to the old man behind the window, I took in all my surroundings. There was a group of ladies in the corner. They all were dressed in short skirts and full make up. One of them had feathers around her neck. I was puzzled because it was not Halloween. On the next bench was an aged woman, who kept nodding, and looking as if she was going to fall on the floor. We were all laughing at her, when I spotted a familiar face. There, across the room, was Aunt Genene. She was in handcuffs, and a female officer was standing next to her.

"Carla, look who's over there," I said.

"Where?" Carla said, looking in the wrong direction.

"Over there, in the handcuffs. It's Aunt Genene," I replied, as I wondered what my uppity Aunt could have done to be at the police station in handcuffs.

I went to the counter to tell Momma. We didn't have to wonder for long, because the female officer left Aunt Genene with another officer, and came to the counter next to Momma.

"Got another one, Pearl," the officer said to the obese lady behind the window.

"What is it this time?" Pearl responded.

"I got a Genene Lila Rock, for changing price tags at J C Penny's. The items she picked out were nice too. She definitely has good taste," laughed the officer.

Momma and I looked at each other, and burst with laughter. I ran over to Carla, to tell her what happened.

"Aunt Genene was changing price tags at Hanes Mall," I boasted.

"Stop gossiping," Momma said, as she came over to the bench.

We burst into laughter all over again.

Our laughter was interrupted by a loud voice. It was Aunt Genene. Unaware of our presence, she proceeded to act a fool. After screaming and jumping up and down, she began reciting nursery rhymes, and biting her handcuffs.

"What is wrong with her?" Mya asked.

"Momma, why she screaming?" Carlos Jr. questioned.

"She's just playing crazy, so she won't go to jail," Momma said.

Aunt Genene's act worked. She ended up getting sent to the mental hospital, instead of jail. Luckily, they had taken her away, just before Daddy came out, and we knew better than to mention it. Without any appreciation, Daddy took the keys from Momma, and led us out the door. He was actually quiet on the ride home. When we reached the house, he instructed us to hurry and get ready for church. I kept getting tickled thinking of Aunt Genene saying nursery rhymes. I was the last one dressed, and Daddy was in the car, blowing as usual.

"Let's go over the song again. I want yall to do it perfect tonight."

We practiced all the way to church. We got there just in time for Daddy to be introduced. He did a James Brown slide across the stage and said, "Let the church say, Amen," like he was not just in jail a few hours prior. He introduced us, and we sang his new song. We did very well, and got a warm response from the congregation.

He went on to preach a stirring sermon, about Daniel being in the lion's den. After rhyming, screaming, and doing a full split, he took off his shoes, and began to walk on the pews. The church was captivated, and cheered him on.

After church, a well-dressed man came up to Momma, and shook her hand. He introduced himself as Mr. Richards. He told her how impressed he was, with our singing.

"They have incredible voices to be so young. Have they ever done any performing?" he said, still holding Momma's hand.

"Only in church," she said, as she backed away from the man. I had tapped her on the arm, after seeing Daddy staring at her, from across the room.

She gathered all the kids, and we headed for the car. Usually Daddy hung around after service, talking with the church members, but not tonight. He was waiting in the car, with a strange look on his face, when we got there. We piled into the car, but Daddy did not drive off. He waited until the last car had pulled off from the church, and then he began.

"Why do you have to be all up in men's faces? I am a pastor, and you disrespected me."

"Carlos, he was only asking me about the children's singing."

As if he did not hear Momma, he said, "Nobody wants you. You got nappy hair and six kids. Who do you think is going to want you?"

"Carlos, please. The kids are tired. Can we please just go home?"

Daddy was in a zone. I don't think he heard anything Momma was saying. He swung at her and missed. This made him really mad, so he pulled her out the car, and threw her to the ground. The beating took place right there, in the dirt parking lot of the church. When the dust cleared Momma was lying in the dirt, motionless again. He drug her to the car, and threw her limp body in the front seat. When we got home, Momma could barely move and Daddy left her in the car.

The next morning Momma was in her bed, and Daddy was gone. I wondered how long he had let her stay out in the car last night. I had wanted to help her out the car, but Daddy instructed us to get in the house and go to bed. I reached out to give her a hug. She flinched when I came into contact with her body and I understood. Carla and I made sure everybody was ready for school, so Momma would not have to get up. We fed and changed Kerry. He was almost potty trained, but we put a diaper on him, so Momma could rest. Before leaving for school, I laid him in the bed with her, and put the television on cartoons. I put some extra juice, two diapers, and some crackers within Momma's reach. I kissed her on the cheek, and ran outside to catch the bus.

"The ride to school seemed long. I was so upset about what happened last night. There were numerous days at school I spent worrying about Momma, and that day was no different. I prayed that Daddy would stay gone all day, and not bother Momma. I also prayed that Kerry would be good today. My teacher caught me daydreaming a couple of times, but I could not help it. There was a lot on my mind for an eleven year old. I wanted her to notice my pain, to see my bruises, and help me. Either the teachers were never aware, or they did not care.

After school, I hurried to the bus. I wanted to get home, and check on Momma. When the bus came to my stop, I jumped down the steps, and ran home. I was happy not to see the old Cadillac. Momma's car was not there either, and that puzzled me. I knew she was hurt, so I couldn't imagine her leaving the house. As I turned my key in the door, thoughts ran through my head. *Momma was pretty bad off when we left. What if she tried to drive herself to the hospital?* Just then I heard Kerry, and rushed to him. He was in my Momma's bedroom. When I reached the door, I saw Momma. She looked like she was in the same spot, we left her in.

"Hey, how are you feeling?" I said.

"I have had better days, baby," Momma said, inviting me to sit on her bed.

"Where's your car?" Mya asked, as she came in the front door.

"Two men came, and one of them drove off in it. I was behind on the payments. Even if I would have had the money, I was too sore to get out of the bed. I just watched them take my car away. There was nothing I could do."

Momma was really hurting, and I became overwhelmed with emotion. "You always tell me to pray and I do. I pray real hard. I'm not trying to rush God, but I am ready to go," I said to her, before bursting into tears.

"I know that we have to leave, but when I do, I will have six children to take care of. Last time I wasn't prepared. I've been trying to put money away for when we leave. It seems like bills keep coming up, that I have to take care of. Your Daddy sure ain't going to make sure their paid."

"Here come Daddy," Carla yelled, as she came in the house.

I kissed Momma, and went into my room to pray that Daddy would be in a good mood. When he came in, he was upset, but not at any of us. He had found out about his sister going to the crazy house. He watered down the story, as he told it to Momma. Mistaken identity was the reason he gave. She never told him what we saw in the police station. She just listened, as he went on and on. I think she was just glad he was angry with someone besides her.

Chapter 13

The house was black as Daddy's old Cadillac when I woke up. I climbed out of bed, and went to the bathroom. When I flipped the switch, nothing happened. I tried it a couple more times before feeling my way to the toilet, and plopping down. Just as I began to use it, I realized the seat was down. A wet stream rolled down my leg. When I stood up, my bare feet met a disgusting puddle. I grabbed the tissue and wiped the toilet lid, my legs, and the floor as best as I could, in the dark. I lifted the seat, and dropped the dripping wad of paper in the toilet. I closed my eyes and prayed, as I reached out to flush. *Yes, the water is still on.* I ran to Momma's room, to inform them of the latest disconnection. As I reached their doorway, I could hear them talking about it already. I went back down the hallway, and got the 'our lights are off again' candles and matches from the closet. I followed our, far to frequent, ritual of placing one or two in every room. At an age when most parents would be telling their kids not to handle matches, I was a match striking pro. When the entire house was glowing, I went back towards Momma's door. Carla was crouched there.

"What are you doing?"

"Be quiet, Sharon." Carla put her hand over my mouth, and pointed to the door. We both listened.

"Carlos, what happened this time? You were supposed to pay the bill."

"Sharon, I will take care of it."

"Why did you give that big offering in church last night, if you knew the bills were not paid? You told me you took care of it."

"I am trying to do the Lord's work. When the Lord says give, that's what I do."

"What did the Lord tell you about these bills?" Momma mumbled.

"What did you say, and who are you to question me?" Daddy shouted.

Carla and I heard a thunderous crash, and then footsteps coming to the door. We sprinted to our room. Daddy came out, slammed the door, and left. When the coast was clear, we ran to Momma's room to see if she was all right. We were shocked to find her sitting on the bed, with a smile on her face.

"Momma are you o.k.?" I asked, thinking that she had gone crazy. "Why are you smiling?"

"Yeah Momma, we heard the loud crash," Carla said.

"Your Daddy was trying to storm out of the room, and tripped on the iron cord. He knocked over the ironing board and the iron. I wish the lights were on, so I could have seen the look on his face. It was so funny."

"I thought he hit you again. I was worried," Carla said.

"I am glad he fell. That's what he get for doing bad stuff to us all the time," I said.

"Now Sharon, that is still your Daddy, and you mind your manners," Carla said with a straight face, and then burst out laughing."

"The Lord should have told him to watch out for that chord," I continued.

This time Momma said, "That's enough Sharon."

We all busted out laughing. The other kids were up by now. They had made the disconnection discovery, and were all piling up in Momma's room.

"Momma, I bumped my knee coming down the hallway, and it hurts," Jason said.

"Look under the sink in the bathroom, and get a band-aid," Momma offered, trying to console him. He still was not happy with Kerry taking his place as Momma's baby, so he needed extra attention.

"These band-aids are big, Momma," Jason hollered from the bathroom.

"Better to heal you with," she laughed.

Just then we heard a knock at the door. We were startled, because we had not heard anybody pull up. Daddy's old Cadillac made a distinctive noise, so we always knew when he was coming.

"Who is it?" Momma called from the doorway.

"It's Jean."

"Oh my God, she must want her money. Not only do I not have it, but now the lights are off." Momma said to herself, but loud enough for me to hear. Momma reluctantly opened the door.

"Jean, I am going to be honest with you. I don't have the money I owe you. In fact I need some more. As you can see the lights are off and…

"Sharon, Daddy is really sick. He is back in the hospital, and really bad off," Aunt Jean interrupted.

Momma was shocked by the news, and began to cry.

"He is in intensive care this time. No one under twelve can go in there. Where is Carlos and why are the lights off again?"

"Carlos stormed out of here this morning. I don't know where he is. The lights are off because he put a hundred dollars in the offering basket instead of the Duke Power drop box," Momma said between sobs.

"Come on Sharon. Get the kids together. I will stay outside the intensive care unit with them, while you visit Daddy. Ma will be glad to see you."

"Thank you Jean. I mean it. Thank you for everything."

"It is the least I could do. I feel so responsible for your situation."

"It's not your fault," Momma said sniffling.

We quickly washed up, and got dressed. Momma made us eat a bowl of cereal. She said the milk would be spoiled, and go to waste, by the time we got back. I was last to leave out the door. I blew all the candles out, and put one by the front door with the matches, in case we came back home at night. As I locked the door, I heard somebody laughing. Momma had just been sad, but even she was smiling. Aunt Jean had noticed a bulge in the knee of Jason's pants. She had his pants pulled down, trying to see what it was.

"Boy, why do you have this in your pants?" Aunt Jean said, peeling off one of our sanitary napkins from his knee.

"I got hurt, and Momma said the big band-aid is better to heal me," Jason said, wondering why everyone was laughing at him.

We were really amused, and laughed all the way to the car. It cheered Momma up a little bit, and she tried to explain to Jason about his mistake. It was hilarious.

"Jean, stop by Ronald's house. Carlos may be there. He can get the kids."

"Are you sure? I don't mind watching them."

"I want to spend some real time with Daddy today."

"Alright, we'll go by there. If he is not there, I will take the kids to my house, so you can have all the time you want. Besides, they have not seen Maurice Jr. in a long time."

Sure enough, Daddy's old Cadillac was parked in front of Ronald's house. We stayed in the car while Momma went to talk to Daddy. I don't know what she said to him, but Daddy came out the house and told us to come inside. We kissed Momma good bye and went inside.

"Did yall speak to Momma?"

"Yes sir," we said in unison.

Daddy was extremely calm and pleasant. He had let Momma go without a fight, and I wondered what was on his mind. He went outside on the front porch, and Ronald followed him.

"Carlos, what did you want to talk to me about?" I overheard Ronald say.

"Dad, I need your help. The lights are off at the house and...

"Again! Boy, didn't I just loan you some money last week. You need to get a job, and take care of your family."

"I work for the Lord."

"You got a wife, and all them children. You need to get yourself together."

Daddy got heated up. He began to yell and scream.

"The Lord is my shepherd, I shall not want."

"There is no reason to get upset. A man is supposed to take care of his family. He supposed to be the head of the household. You know what you need to do."

"What about you? How many households are you trying to be the head of, you dirty dog!"

"Carlos, you get off my porch and get the hell out of here!"

"My brother wasn't in the ground good, before you helped yourself to his household! You know you are wrong for sleeping with that poor lady. You got her and them kids over there terrorized," Daddy continued.

"I will get my gun, and blow your darn head off if you don't get off my property!"

Daddy leaped off the porch, and ran into the street. As we watched from the window, Daddy began to jump up and down. He took his shirt off and threw it on the ground, this continued until he only had on his underwear and socks. He walked back and forth up the street preaching.

"Take me to Genene! I want to go where Genene is!"

I could not believe what was happening. Daddy was in the middle of the street with his clothes off, asking to go to the crazy house. Uncle Timothy had pulled up, and was in the street trying to make him stop. He had been so calm before. I always used to hear the quote 'the sea is always calmest before the storm'. Now I fully understood what that meant. Someone must have called the police, because we started hearing sirens. The closer they got, the louder Daddy got. Upon arrival, the policeman surveyed the scene, and called for back up. When three officers could not get him to settle down, they arrested Daddy.

In true Porter fashion, Ronald forgot he was mad at Daddy, and came to his defense. Uncle Timothy got so mad he spit on one of the officers, and they arrested him too. The officers put Daddy and Uncle Timothy in separate cars, and sped off. Ronald took off behind them. Grandma Florida, who had been watching the whole thing, had called over to the hospital and told Momma what was going on.

When Momma got there, we were ready to go. We had found Daddy's keys in the street, and gave them to Momma. She thanked Grandma, told Aunt Jean good bye, and we left to go home. After Momma had told us about Grandpa's worsening condition, we tried to tell her what happened.

"Daddy took his clothes off, Momma," Jason shrieked.

Everyone was trying to tell the story at once.

"Ronald say Daddy need a job," Carlos Jr. said

"Daddy said Ronald's helping himself to Uncle Bud's household," Carla said.

That comment made Momma do a double take.

"Did Carlos really say that? Did Mrs. Florida hear him?"

"Yes, and she said, "a piece a man, is better than no man.""

"That is one crazy family," Momma said.

"Pizza man," Kerry mocked from the back seat.

Carla and I cracked up. Kerry was trying to talk more and more everyday. We were in a good mood all the way home, until we pulled up in the driveway. The yellow piece of paper, with a big staple in the center, jerked us back into reality. Grandpa was sick, Daddy was in jail, the lights were cut off, and now we were being evicted, for the third time in my short life. As she walked up the steps, Momma snatched down the notice. I hoped Nicki had not seen it. She would pick at us for sure, and the whole school would know.

After relighting all the candles, we went to our rooms. Momma had asked that we give her a few minutes of quiet time. She said she needed to think. Carla and I went in the kitchen to see what we could fix for dinner. The tomatoes and rice we ate at Ronald's, was long gone from our stomachs. We found some bologna, but the mayonnaise had turned yellow from the refrigerator not being on. We had a lovely candlelight dinner of dry bologna sandwiches, and hot Kool-Aid. I took Momma a plate, but she said she was not hungry. After dinner, we all sat in a circle in the boy's room and told ghost stories. Carlos Jr. had told a really scary story, so naturally we all jumped, when we heard the doorknob turning.

"Get up and get ready for church," Daddy said.

I don't know how, but Daddy never stays in jail. He always gets out quick. There he was standing in the doorway smiling at us, like he was not naked in the street earlier.

Chapter 14

Just as we were getting put out of our house, Aunt Genene was being let out of the crazy house. She had escaped jail time and a criminal record. Just like with Aunt Tangerine's situation, the family quickly brushed it under the rug and moved on. It would not come up again, unless someone got mad at the other. Daddy did not have a place for us to go, so we moved to Aunt Genene's cold basement. I was very embarrassed. I did not want to have to go back to school with Francis. The thought of her making fun of me made me sick to my stomach. All I ever wanted was for her to like me. Even though I was young, I knew that family was not supposed to hurt each other. *Why were people in Daddy's family, including Daddy, always hurting me?*

Our second day there, Aunt Genene decided that me, Carla, and Mya had the nappiest hair she'd ever seen. She went to the store, and bought three boxes of Jherri Curl, and a big jar of activator. She called Aunt Brenda over, and they proceeded to put Jherri Curls in our hair, with their untrained hands. Francis and Mona thought it was the funniest thing. They walked back and forth through the kitchen giggling and pointing. Neither of my Aunts made them stop. We were humiliated. The end result was a Jherri straight, because we did not have one curl in our heads. I wondered why Momma let them do that to us, but I wasn't mad at her. She was busy nursing a busted lip, because we had a revival in two days. Momma was always hiding bruises and scars. She had an old makeup compact that she kept for that very reason. It was real sad that the only time Momma made up her face was to cover up something.

I was so happy on day three, when the church blessed Daddy with a rental house that they utilized for their outreach ministry. It was only a two bedroom, but I didn't care. We moved all our stuff in one day. We got the biggest room, since once again all six of us had to share a bedroom. The house had a fireplace and we were really excited about that. It was three weeks until Christmas, and we finally would get to hang stockings for the first time.

We had missed a couple days, so Momma quickly got us enrolled in yet another school. The worst part of moving around was always being the nappy headed new kid with second hand clothes. Always being picked last for the kickball teams, and never having money for the field trips, was not good either. Where most kids would be excited about school trips, they always made me cringe. I knew that Momma would look at the permission slip, and not be able to afford it. I would conveniently stay out of school that day. On some occasions, the school would have a special fund, and I would get to go.

Momma had been really quiet lately. I think she was worried about Grandpa or growing tired of Daddy's mess. She did not decorate the house, as she had in the past. We had been there a couple of days, and still had sheets up to the window.

"Momma are you o.k.?" I asked one day after school. The dried up tears she wore on her face, were a dead give away that something was wrong.

"Baby, my Dad is gone home, and I did not get to say good bye. I feel like my whole life is slipping away. I want to be with him. What has become of my life."

Even though Carla was the oldest, Momma and I always had a special connection, and for some reason she would always confide in me. Today, however, I was not prepared for her blunt dialogue. She sounded like she was giving up.

"Momma you always tell us to pray. You gotta believe that God will help us."

Without responding, Momma put her head in my lap. She laid there and cried. I did not know what to do. I wanted to make her smile again. I looked up to God and prayed.

"Lord please help us. Please give us a way out. We sing this song in church that says 'he wouldn't have brought you this far, just, to leave you'. Please don't leave us Lord. We need you. Momma needs you. Amen."

"Amen," I heard. I was startled to hear voices in the room, and looked up to see Carla and Mya.

They came over and joined us on the couch.

"Momma, we love you, and we want you to be happy," Carla said.

"I am sorry for making you guys worry about me. I loved my Dad so much, and he is gone. I missed a lot of time with him, and so did you all."

Momma was right. Other than at the hospital, I could not remember any interactions with Grandpa. I couldn't remember a conversation or Sunday dinner or anything. Who was George Eli Johnson, I would never know. That really hurt.

"Was he a nice Daddy? Did he hit Grandma Mary?" Mya asked.

"He was the best. He never hit my Mom, and only whipped us if we did something really bad."

"I wish Daddy was nice. He always seems so angry," Carla said.

Sanedria Arne Potter

"Listen girls, the next couple of days I need you all to be on your best behavior. I refuse to go to my Dad's funeral with bruises on me, or you all."

"Yes ma'am."

We had eaten dinner by the time Daddy made it home. Momma went straight into the kitchen, and warmed up his plate. She did not even ask him where he had been. As he ate his food, Momma sat down at the table with him.

"Carlos, today my Dad lost his battle with Alzheimer's. I want to go over to Ma's house and be with my family."

"I am your family. I need you here. Besides, we have church tonight."

"Carlos, my Dad died today."

"I heard you the first time. You can go to the funeral, but you don't need to be sitting around over there with all those cackling hens."

I could not believe my Daddy. How could he be so mean? Momma must have been devastated. But the fear of having a black eye at the funeral kept her quiet. I ran down

154

the hallway to our bedroom. We had two sets of bunk beds and a single bed crammed in the room. I got in my bed and put the covers over my head. *I have to do something. This has to stop.* The thoughts raced through my head. *I want to kill Daddy. Will they send an eleven year-old to jail? Would Daddy haunt me in my sleep?* I drifted off to sleep. I had just begun a dream that involved Daddy being ran over by his own Cadillac. The driver of the car was just about to be revealed, when the covers were jerked off of me. When I opened my eyes, Daddy was standing over me, with a crazy look in his eyes. *Did he know what I was dreaming about?*

"Why are you in the bed? You know that we have church. Get your butt out of that bed."

"Yes sir," I said, as I jumped out of the bed and began to get ready for church.

Chapter 15

Grandpa's funeral was on a Friday. We were allowed to stay home from school. Momma had obeyed Daddy, and not gone to be with her family. For that reason, she was really anxious to get to the funeral home. Daddy had announced that he had some witnessing to do, and would not be attending. He had left the house earlier. This left Momma with no ride and no support from her husband during her time of grief.

"Carla, go next door and ask if you can use the phone. Call Jean and tell her we need a ride."

Carla ran next door, while I helped Momma get everything ready. A few minutes later she came back and said the phone keep ringing. I could see the tears welling up in Momma's eyes, as she put the clip-on necktie on Kerry.

"One of you finish getting Kerry ready."

Without waiting for a response, she ran into her bedroom. The tears she tried to hide were freely flowing down her face. At that moment, I felt so bad for her. If we missed Grandpa's funeral, Momma might not recover. The weeping was loud enough for everyone to hear now, so I ran to her bedroom. Upon entering, I saw coins all over her bed. There were pennies, dimes, nickels, quarters and even some fifty-cent pieces. There were a few folded up bills as well.

"Tell Carla to use the phone again, and call a cab. Then come back in here, and help me count this money."

Momma's words were barely audible through her sobbing, but I understood. I delivered the message, and returned to help count out the coins.

"My pile comes to four dollars and fifty cents, without the pennies. How much do you have, Momma?"

"I have three ones and two five's. That makes a total of seventeen dollars and fifty cents."

"Do we have enough?

"I hope so, baby."

"Grandma Florida gave me a quarter the last time I was there. I've been saving it, but you can have it."

"Thank you. I don't know what I would do without you kids."

Carla ran in the house, and announced that the cab would be there in ten minutes. We rarely rode cabs, because they were expensive. The ride was timed, so we scrambled to make sure we would be ready as soon as the driver pulled up. Momma gave all of us a once over. She just shook her head at our straight hair. The only thing we could do with it was slick it back.

"The cabs here," Jason yelled moments later.

Everyone ran out the door, and piled into the yellow vehicle. The bearded old man looked surprised to see so many of us.

"We need to go to Ryan's Funeral Home on Old Greensboro Road."

"Yes Ma'am," he responded.

During the ride, Momma was in deep thought. She was quiet, and staring out the window. Jason and I had sat in the front seat, and when I happened to glance at the meter it was almost at seventeen dollars, and we were still a couple of blocks from the funeral home.

"Momma, look at the meter," I said.

By the time she raised up to look it was at seventeen dollars and rolling. Frustration filled her face, as she thought about the amount of money she had.

"You can let us out right up here," she said pointing to the corner of Old Greensboro Road and Waterworks Road. The driver slowed down, and pulled up on the curb, so we would not be in the street.

"That will be seventeen dollars and seventy cents."

Momma scooped all of the change out of her coat pocket and the folded up bills out of her purse. I proudly handed her my quarter, which I had brought just in case she needed it. The driver frowned, as Momma handed him all that change. Paying him no mind, she got out of the cab, and instructed all of us to get on the sidewalk. When we were all out, she closed the door, and straightened out her dress.

"Hey Sharon," Momma said.

"Yes Ma'am."

"Catch this," she said, and threw me the nickel, she had left from the cab fare.

We all grabbed each others hand, and made the one mile journey to the funeral home.

How can Momma deal with this? I always asked myself that question, because I could not understand. The next thing I knew, the sound of an upbeat song we sang in church was being belted out. One by one we all joined in. We marched down the street, singing as loud as we could. When we reached the funeral home, Momma paused at the front door, and took a deep breath. She opened the doors of the chapel, and led us up the aisle to the open casket at the front. Grandpa looked different than I remembered. He looked swollen. I stared at him for a long time. The urge to reach out and touch him was strong, but I was scared. Momma openly wept in front of the casket. She looked like she was going to pass out. I guess Uncle Teddy saw what I saw, because he came and tried to take Kerry from her arms, but he would not let go.

"My Mama said no," he screamed. "No strangers."

I quickly grabbed Kerry, and we went to sit down beside Grandma Mary on the front row. Although he was our Uncle, Kerry had never seen him before. Momma started crying even harder. I think the fact that we did not get to know Grandpa, and Kerry did not know Uncle Teddy, hurt her even more. My heart ached for her, because she was crying so hard. Eventually, the usher had to take her out to get some air. As she walked down the aisle, you could hear her pain.

The funeral was nice. Momma came back about halfway through the service. She sat on the pew, and rocked back and forth. We watched as a few of Grandpa's old coworkers had words. They all had good things to say about him. I felt like I needed to take notes, so I could remember what he was like.

"Praise the Lord everybody," we heard come from the back of the chapel. I don't know if the last speaker had finished, but he awkwardly smiled and sat down.

"Praise the Lord," the people that did not know Daddy was crazy responded.

Daddy slid up the aisle, and grabbed the microphone. He sang a song, and then began to preach. Daddy just took over the funeral. The director ended up turning on the overhead music to drown him out. When he finally calmed down, he came to the front row. Daddy scooped Kerry up, and sat in his place. I could see Grandma Mary peering at him for the rest of the funeral, with pure hate in her eyes. If looks could kill, we would have had another funeral that day.

It had started raining really hard, while we were inside the funeral home, so we could not go to the graveyard. Grandma announced that everyone was going back to her house. Daddy announced that we would not be going, and grabbed Momma by the arm, and led her to the old Cadillac. I waved good bye to Grandma from the backseat of the car. I waved, until I could not see her anymore. Momma was in a zombie like state. She was quiet, and doing her normal rocking. Every now and then she would mumble something. I had no idea what she was saying. I think she had finally been pushed over the edge. The thought of being left with Daddy, without her, was a terrifying thought.

When we got home, we knew to go and take off our good clothes. As I was changing, I overheard Daddy say. "Don't think I didn't see all those men hugging on you. I have told you numerous times that I am the only one who will have you. Don't nobody want no used up, nappy headed woman, with six kids. You are worthless. You hear me."

"Carlos, today was my Daddy's funeral. Don't you have any compassion."

Daddy answered her with a backhand across the face, followed by a blow to the stomach. He saw us watching, and ordered us to go to bed even though it was daylight. As I lay in my bed and listened to Momma's screams, I knew that something had to be done. Mya suggested that we get the knives out of the kitchen, and cut him up.

"We only have two knives, Mya," Carla said. "Why don't we set him on fire, like he did Momma?"

"We have to do something before he kills Momma, and then has to raise us alone," Carlos Jr. said.

"I got my baseball bat," Jason said too loudly.

"Shhh. Do you want Daddy to hear you," I said trying to think of a way to get rid of Daddy. Whatever we decided, it had to be done while he was asleep, because we were all too afraid to confront him face to face. We all went to sleep, and decided to tell Momma about our discussion in the morning.

We did not get the chance to tell her anything. At about 5:25 in the morning, Momma was whispering in my ear telling me to get up. Daddy was sound asleep. He must have been very exhausted, since he had been yelling, throwing things, and fighting with Momma all night. We were once again sneaking out of the house, carrying what little we could with us. Momma was leaving Daddy again, but we were not as excited as before. We knew that it was only a matter of time, before he found us, and we would be right back where we started. I thought, we couldn't just leave. My mind told me elimination was the only way.

"Hurry up yall, and be quiet," I told them. "We don't want to wake up Daddy."

The younger ones immediately became quiet as mice. They knew what waking up Daddy would mean. Momma was frantic, and limping. Daddy had given her a beat down like no other. One of her eyes was completely closed. Her mouth was swollen so much, she reminded me of JJ on Good Times. She had several, very visible, scratches on her face and neck. Her hair was all over her head, although that was normal.

Momma was mumbling to herself. I'm not positive, but I thought I heard " I ain't taking this shit no more!"

I hoped that was what she said. I just know that I was fed up with Daddy, and all that craziness.

We walked up the street to the bus stop, with Momma looking behind us every few minutes. I just said a prayer that God would let Daddy sleep until we were long gone. The bus came while Momma was trying to count pennies for bus fare. It was all we had, and my nickel. We all piled on, tired and sleepy. The bus driver looked at the bag of pennies, and Momma's lip. He must have sensed that we were in a bad situation, because he said "Ma'am just pay for yourself, and find your kids some seats."

Momma thanked him and we all went to the back of the bus, and sat down. She let out a big sigh, but I wasn't feeling any relief yet. We got downtown, and changed buses.

"Where are we going?" I asked

"Somewhere safe and quiet, baby," she responded.

After a few minutes, she pushed the bell for us to get off. We were in front of what looked like a mansion. It was a really big brick house, with a fence around it. We walked up to the gate, and Momma pressed a button on it.

A sleepy voice said, "May I help you?"

Momma answered that she was out there with her six children, and she needed help. A tall white lady let us in. After talking with Momma in her office, she led us to a room with two beds in it. She brought us some extra blankets and a snack. Momma sang us a song, prayed and put us to bed. Me, Mya and Carla slept on the floor while Momma, the baby and the boys took the beds.

When I awoke it was after 3 p.m., and I was in the room alone. I stretched, and got up to look for everyone. They were in the kitchen eating peanut butter sandwiches, and drinking milk. Momma gave me a hug, and told me to sit down and eat. Everyone actually looked happy. Mya was humming some weird little tune, and my brothers were poking and pushing each other. After we ate, we all went back to the room.

"Yall sit down, so I can talk to you," Momma said. "We are going to be staying here for awhile. That means you all will go to school from here. You are not to tell anyone where we are staying. If someone asks questions, then tell them to talk to me. You are not to leave school, or go anywhere with your father if you should see him. Do you understand me?"

"Yes ma'am," we all said in unison.

"Mama are we really not going to live with Daddy anymore?" Jason asked.

"You all deserve a better life than what you were living and I deserve better as well. Your father has beat me down long enough. He needs some serious help. I refuse to subject you all to that anymore."

The next day was Sunday, and we went to a service in the chapel at the shelter. This service was very different from the ones we had with Daddy. We sat very quiet and listened. A hymn was sung, and a man stood up and talked for about ten minutes. We said a prayer, and it was over.

"Was that all?" I asked.

"Yes, Sharon."

"Well, I like this church," said Carla.

Mama smiled and said, "That's good, baby."

We went to the recreation room downstairs. There were a few other children there and a lady with a teenage girl. Momma sat down beside the lady, and extended her hand. "Hi, I'm Sharon."

"Hello, my name is Janice, and this is my daughter Princess."

"Nice to meet you both, these are my children Carla, Sharon, Mya, Carlos, Jason, and my baby boy, Kerry."

"Wow," said Janice, "You must have a lot of patience."

"That and God," Momma said.

We went off to play, while she and Mrs. Janice sat and talked.

****

The following morning, we went to register at a new school. We would attend Ardmore Elementary. I liked my teacher. Her name was Mrs. Ingram. She had had a talk with Momma, and was immediately very nice to me. She asked me if I wanted to stand up and tell the class about myself. I was horrified. If I told them anything about me, I was sure to be picked on every day.

I said, "No ma'am."

She looked at me, sort of confused and her expression changed.

"Oh honey, just tell us your name, age, and what you like to do."

I stood up and said, " My name is Sharon. I am 11 years old, and I like to play with my brothers and sisters."

The whole class said, "Hi, Sharon."

My first day was going great until lunchtime. I walked into the cafeteria and froze. I hadn't brought a lunch, and Momma hadn't given me any money, or told me what to do. Slowly, I moved to the end of the line. After my class had gone through, I just sat down at a table with them. Mrs.

Ingram looked up, and noticed that I had no food. She came towards me. *Oh my God, I am going to be embarrassed, what am I going to say?*

"Sharon, why are you not eating?" asked Mrs. Ingram.

"Umm, I'm not hungry," I lied.

" Come and let me talk to you a moment." I got up and walked over to the corner with her.

"What's wrong, honey?"

" I don't have any money and I didn't bring a lunch."

" Well you need to eat, lets get you some food. I will give you a form to take home to your mother."

"Thank you," I said.

I sat down and ate the best grilled cheese sandwich and tator tots I had ever had. The rest of the day went quickly.

When I returned to the shelter, I began to tell Carla and Mya about my day. I was so excited.

"Things are going to be different this time y'all."

"Hope you are right, Sharon," Carla said.

" Me too," Mya shrieked.

Momma came in the room and said "Hey girls, how was your first day at school."

We all started talking at once. "Whoa, wait a minute, I can't hear you all at the same time. Just hold on, I have some good news. After I tell you my news, then we will talk about your day. I got a job today."

"Ooh Momma, for real," I said

"That was quick, where'd you find one?" Mya asked.

"It is called Hanes Hosiery, it is a factory that sews and make clothes, underwear, and hosiery."

"You are great at making things," Carla said.

"Thank you baby, I start on Friday so I have to get prepared. Let's go get your brothers and get something to eat."

Chapter 16

Momma began working at her new job. She said that she loved it. We got a few new things. Getting new clothes and shoes, were always a big deal. Momma found a great church, and within a week we were members. Momma joined the choir, and immediately started to lead songs. It was so good to see her finally looking happy. I felt like I could finally breath a sigh of relief.

A month had passed and life was wonderful. We had a routine, and we were all doing well. We were still in the same city as Daddy, so in the back of our heads we knew we had to be careful. Momma said, he would never think that we were right here in the city. But with no money, this was as far as we could have gone. Although she hated to, she did not tell anyone where we were, not even her Mom.

I overheard her making a phone call. She called Grandma Mary and simply stated, "The kids and I are fine. I will call you back when it is safe and tell you where we are."

It was Monday afternoon, and we had just gotten home from school. Momma was sitting in the recreation room with Mrs. Janice and an older white lady named Penny. Mrs. Penny was elderly, but her husband was still abusing her.

Momma turned when we came in. "Hey guys, I gotta tell you something. We are moving out of here soon."

My heart sank. I thought, *Oh God, Daddy found us.*

"No, I don't want to go back," I cried. "I am happy here."

"No, no, no," she said, jumping up. " That is not what I meant honey, come here." She gave me a big hug.

"You mean we're not going back," Carla said.

"No way, sweetie. We are through with that chapter of our life. I was trying to tell you guys that I found us a house."

"A house? Our own house," Jason shouted."

"Yes baby that is exactly what I mean. A three bedroom house in a nice neighborhood, with a backyard and everything."

We were very excited, and everyone was hugging and jumping up and down.

"When are we moving?" Carla asked.

"In about two weeks," she said. "Oh yeah, Carla, Mrs. Penny wants to know if you could go downtown with her, so that she can take care of some business. She may need you to help carry some things.

"Yes ma'am," Carla replied.

"Can I go too?" I asked.

"Sure," Mrs. Penny said.

Carla and I hurried to put away our bookbags and get ready to leave.

"We are ready," I announced a short while later.

"Please behave girls," Momma instructed.

"Yes ma'am," we said as we ran out the door.

The three of us got on the city bus, and headed for downtown. I was looking out the window at all the people and places we were passing. When we got to town, Mrs.

Penny said, "You guys stay with me okay and don't go running off."

"Sure thing, Mrs. Penny," we chimed, excited to be downtown.

Mrs. Penny went to the courthouse, she said she had some papers to sign. Then we went to the pawnshop, where a man gave her forty dollars for her wedding ring. We went in a department store called Woolworth's. She bought a few things for herself, and some candy for us.

When we were about to leave, Mrs. Penny said, "looks like it is going to rain." So she went back and bought an umbrella. We walked back up the street to the bus stop. I loved downtown. There were all kinds of clothing stores and shoe stores. I looked in the windows, and imagined being able to go inside and pick out whatever I wanted. We sat down on one of the benches. No sooner than I sat down I heard a familiar voice shouting, or rather preaching. I stood up to look at where the commotion was coming from. There, on the other side of the walkway, was my Daddy jumping up and down, and shouting the word of God. Right at that moment, he looked over and saw me. He came walking toward me, and I sat down quickly.

"What's the matter honey?" said Mrs. Penny.

I didn't say anything, because I was scared. Daddy walked up, and looked around. He didn't see anybody he knew close by, so he knelt in front of me.

"Hey baby," he said and hugged me.

"Hey Daddy," I responded, wondering where Carla had gone.

I felt Mrs. Penny flinch.

"How you doing Sharon?"

"Fine Daddy."

"What are you doing downtown by yourself?"

"Excuse me, she's with me," Mrs. Penny said, after mustering up some courage.

"Who are you?" asked Daddy.

"A friend of their Mothers."

"Come here Carla, and let me talk to you," he said, after noticing that she was hovering in the crowd that was gathering. Carla did not move.

He grabbed my hand, and pulled me up.

"No! She is not going anywhere with you!"

"What did you say?" Daddy shouted.

"I said she is not going anywhere with you. Her mother left her in my care, and she is staying right here!"

"You don't tell me what I can do with my daughters. I don't know where my wife is with my kids, and then I see my daughters' downtown with some white woman. You can't tell me I can't talk to my children. God gave me these children. Come on Sharon." He grabbed my arm again.

"No!" Mrs. Penny screamed. "Leave her alone." Mrs. Penny started swinging her umbrella. "Leave her alone. Somebody call the police."

I was very scared, and embarrassed. I didn't know what to do. Everyone was looking, and Mrs. Penny was yelling, and crying. Daddy was yelling, and preaching. Carla still did not move from the crowd. *He gonna make Mrs. Penny have a heart attack.* Even though I was scared, I was certain that I was not going anywhere with Daddy.

Soon we began to hear sirens. Two squad cars pulled up. The first car had two young officers. The second car to arrive had one large, tall man.

"What's going on here?" one of the young officers said.

"These are my children in Jesus name, and you, nor your sirens, nor your guns are gonna take that from me."

As Daddy went on and on, the tall officer went over to talk to Mrs. Penny.

"What seems to be the problem?"

"We live at the Battered Women's Shelter on 5th Street, and their Momma let them come shopping with me. He does not know where they are. This is his first time seeing them since Sharon left him," Mrs. Penny whispered.

"Sir, I am only going to ask you one more time to calm down," the young officer pleaded.

"I will not calm down. God is on my side."

The two young officers got on either side of Daddy, and tried to restrain him.

Just then the bus came, and the tall officer instructed us to get on. That really set things off.

"Mrs. Penny, where is Carla?" I asked.

The crowd had grown, and we could no longer see her.

"Carla," Mrs. Penny called out. She and the tall officer were wading through the crowd trying to find her. I just sat on the bus, and watched the scene. Daddy was fighting like he really cared about us. Some of the people in the crowd were on his side, and yelling at the police. The two officers were having trouble controlling him, and wrestled with him for a while before ending up on the ground. One of the young officers landed on the bottom of the pile. Next was Daddy, then the other officer. The one on the bottom was trying to get up, and pushed Daddy in the face. Before he could move his hand, Daddy had caught one of his fingers, and clamped down on it. The officer screamed, while the other officer put his nightstick around Daddy's neck, and began to choke him. The more pressure he applied, the harder Daddy bit down. The officers piercing screams caught the attention of the tall officer. He rushed over, and started spraying pepper spray straight into Daddy's eyes. Amazingly it had no effect on him. Maybe his Vietnam days had made him immune to chemicals. He kept on biting down, apparently unaltered. When they were finally able to rescue the finger from his mouth, it appeared to be hanging off. *He had almost bit another human's finger off.* Mrs. Penny and Carla boarded the bus, and we left, just as they were putting Daddy in the squad car.

"Where were you scaredy cat?"

"Don't act like you wasn't scared, Sharon."

" I might have been scared, but I wasn't going with him."

"Me either. Wait till I tell Momma."

Just then I looked over at Mrs. Penny. She was white as a ghost. I think today was a bit much for her. She was quiet all the way home. As the bus pulled up to the corner, we gathered Mrs. Penny's bags, and stood on the steps. When the doors opened, we jumped down the steps, and ran into the shelter.

"Momma, Momma, Daddy was downtown, and he tried to take us, and Mrs. Penny beat him with her umbrella," I rattled off without taking a breath.

"Daddy was fighting the police, and he bit one of their fingers off," Carla added.

We were about finished telling the story, when Mrs. Penny made it through the door. She looked exhausted. Momma went up to her, and apologized.

"I know that look on your face, all too well. I am so sorry that you had to go through that," she offered as she hugged Mrs. Penny, and walked her to her room. We told her we would bring her bags up for her.

As soon as they left the room Mya said, "What happened again?"

"Girl, Daddy was going crazy. Three officers could not handle him."

"Shut up Carla. How would you know, you were too busy hiding."

"Whatever, Sharon."

We laughed about Daddy for a long time. Everytime we described the scene, Mya and Carlos Jr. would crack up all over again.

"That's enough yall," Momma said, when she returned from calming Mrs. Penny down. "I know things seem comfortable to you, but you gotta realize, that now Carlos knows that we are still in Winston. Your Daddy is not somebody you play with. I am determined not to go back. I will not subject you all or myself to that kind of life anymore. Tomorrow I will get a restraining order, but that will help only so much.

"But they took him to jail, Momma," Carla said.

"Do you know how many times he's been arrested. I don't know how, but he always gets out. He is never there for more than a few days. He will probably be out tomorrow."

The room was suddenly very quiet. You could hear a pin drop. We all sat there; having been brought back to reality.

Momma said, "Don't look so sad. We just have to stick together, and we will be all right. Going back is not an option. We're going to make it!"

Things that make you go hmmmmm…

➤ Is Sharon Porter able to stay strong and make a life for her children?

➤ What happens with Elder Carlos Porter?

➤ Whatever became of Bernice and her baby?

➤ Does Aunt Tangerine ever get any help?

➤ Where is Francis Rock?

➤ What's going on with Grandma Florida and her 'piece a man', Ronald?

Stay tuned for the next book by Sanedria Arne Potter that picks up where "Behind The Pulpit" left off.

Revisit your favorite and not so favorite characters.

About The Author

Sanedria Arne Potter was born June 7th, 1974 in Winston-Salem, NC. She was the second oldest of six children. Her father was a Vietnam Veteran turned Preacher. Her mother was a Seamstress and a homemaker. They moved around to several cities throughout the North Carolina area. This caused Sanedria to be the new kid 9 different times, at 9 different schools, in her Elementary School career. It was during these difficult times that she began to write.

Her mother and father divorced after 13 years of marriage, and Sanedria finally began a somewhat normal existence. Throughout her life, writing has always helped her get through the tough days. The writing of "Behind The Pulpit" was something she felt she had to do. She wanted people, young and old, to know that you can overcome anything. She also wanted to raise awareness that there are a lot of Veterans that are still struggling to cope.

Sanedria finished school in 1992, and began work as a Collections Analyst. She later left that job and became a 911 Operator. Wanting more out of life, Sanedria moved to

Atlanta, Ga. at the age of 24. She only knew one person when she moved there, but she was determined to make it.

Today at age 29, Sanedria Arne Potter is a Real Estate Investor, and the owner of a Real Estate Appraisal Company. Being self-employed was a lifetime dream for her. It allows her a lot of free time to write. She is currently working on her next book that picks up where "Behind The Pulpit" left off. When she is not writing, she is busy trying to keep up with her two-year-old son, Jaelen. The two of them currently reside in Atlanta, Ga.

About The Book

Behind The Pulpit is a revealing look at the life of a young girl, whose Dad is a Vietnam Veteran turned Preacher. Many soldiers returned from Vietnam with serious issues and Elder Carlos Porter was no exception. Unable to control the vivid images of war or the emptiness of being forgotten by his country, Porter controlled the one thing he felt he could…his family. From severe beatings to monitoring the way food was chewed, Porter ruled with an iron fist. This book is the untold story of life with a Vietnam Dad, told from his 9-year-old daughter's point of view.

www.ingramcontent.com/pod-product-compliance
Lightning Source LLC
Chambersburg PA
CBHW030321290526
45785CB00001B/460